Fast-Track Secrets
for
Making Your Business
Saleable!

by

LORRAINE MCGREGOR
ROB MCGREGOR

ISBN 0-7414-6892-1

Printed in the United States of America

Published November 2011

INFINITY PUBLISHING
1094 New DeHaven Street, Suite 100
West Conshohocken, PA 19428-2713
Toll-free (877) BUY BOOK
Local Phone (610) 941-9999
Fax (610) 941-9959
Info@buybooksontheweb.com
www.buybooksontheweb.com

Quick Response Code

Do you want to learn more about how to make your business saleable?

If you have a phone with a camera, scan this code with your free iPhone 'Paperlinks' app or Android apps: Google Goggles, Zxing or Kaywa. Symbian users can use the barcode scanner provided and Maemo users can use 'mbarcode'. Blackberry users will pick up the code automatically.

No camera phone?

Go to www.MakeYourBusinessSaleable.com!

Disclaimer

The information contained in this document is subject to change without notice, and it represents the current view of the author(s).

Complying with all applicable copyright laws is the responsibility of the user. Without limiting the rights under copyright, you may not reproduce any part of this document, store or introduce any content contained herein into a retrieval system, transmit in any form or by any means (electronic, mechanical, photocopying, recording or otherwise), or for any purpose without the express written permission of the author(s).

The information contained in this document is proprietary and the exclusive property of the author(s), except as otherwise indicated.

The information in this document provides content for discussion and general informational purposes only. The author(s) MAKE NO REPRESENTATIONS, WARRANTIES, EXPRESS, IMPLIED OR STATUTORY, REGARDING THE INFOR-MATION IN THIS DOCUMENT. Nothing in this document constitutes investment, accounting, tax or legal advice. The reader is solely responsible for any use or application of the information or results achieved from the content. The author(s) advise you to seek appropriate investment, accounting, tax, legal and other professional advice regarding your applicable jurisdictions, prior to acting or relying on any of the strategies in this book.

The case studies included in this book are based on our client files. Names, numbers, strategies and defining features have been changed, and some of the characters are composites of several people.

All of the achieved results are factual.

Table of Contents

Acknowledgements

To the people who take the big risks to own businesses and employ so many, thank you for serving as the backbone of our economy. You make our cities and towns thriving, liveable communities for us all.

Testimonials

"Every private client advisor (or wealth advisor, relationship manager) should provide their clients who own a business, a copy of this extraordinary book . . . this book is a fantastic breakthrough resource for preparing to sell your business at maximum value. If your client owns a business, they need to have this book . . . they will thank you endlessly and never move their wealth to another advisor."

Thomas R. Sweet, Former VP Consumer Marketing, City National Bank, Beverly Hills, CA and Former VP Marketing, Nevada State Bank

---

"Supply and demand are critical to every business owner. You started your business to be able to supply a product, or service, to fill a need in your marketplace. Once you start to plan to sell your business it's the SAME thing! You will need to once again become part of the supply-demand chain and if you are not properly prepared, the buyers will quickly move on to a business that is. It's your choice. No, it's your responsibility . . . to actively and aggressively plan for that date one day when you will be ready to sell out to the best possible buyer at the best possible price."

Randy West, Certified Financial Planner, The Villages, Florida

"In my view, to maximize enterprise value, the key thing the seller needs to have sorted before they start a process to sell their business is to have thought through and implemented an organizational structure that does not include them. Too many times in small owner-managed businesses, the roles and responsibilities are not well defined and, ultimately, every key decision comes to the owner or his right hand person. That is not a scalable business model which sophisticated buyers will see; and, thus, feel the need to bring on additional management resources which is an additional cost to the business."

Martin B. Carsky, CEO Con-Space Communications, Ltd and former EVP, Anthem Capital

———————————

"Insightful! What a great roadmap for maximizing the sale of a business. As a business lawyer, we often see overwhelming challenges for business owners who do not prepare for the sale in advance. An ounce of prevention is worth a pound of cure and there is a ton of information in this book that will help sellers quickly turn their business into one that is 'saleable.'

I plan on recommending this book to every client who is thinking about selling a business or even just starting a business and wants to build it right from the start. Not only will it make business owners smarter about selling a business, it will make them smarter about running a business!"

Roger P. Glovsky, Esq. Venture Attorney, Indigo Venture Law Offices and founder of the Seminar - "How to Save Thousands of Dollars on Legal and Professional Fees by Preparing *in Advance* for the Sale of a Business"

"Fast-Track Secrets for Making Your Business Saleable is an outstanding roadmap every owner or manager selling a business will want, to control the process and maximize returns. Suitable for any type of business, this step-by-step approach teaches the business and mindset requirements for success, including 'what you don't know that you don't know' which can jeopardize results. Buy this book if you want maximum profits and peace of mind!"

Susan Rosenthal, President World Markets Group, Former Vice President, Global Marketing CitiBusiness™ for Citigroup

---

"Just like bookends! In my own book, I claim that a small business is no more than a job unless the owner has it positioned to be sold. Now, along come Lorraine and Rob with all of the steps to do precisely that! This is a great addition to any business owner's library."

Roger McManus, Publisher, Ensanity Press

INTRODUCTION

Think about this for a second – how will your life change, knowing you can sell your business when you want and for the price you desire? Do you think that certainty would affect your happiness, health and lifestyle? Here's another thing to think about – if you have a plan in place for the transition of ownership of your business at the point of sale, how will that affect your employees? How will your family feel, knowing they will have a more secure financial future? What if you learn that the work of making your company saleable will actually produce better profits?

They're interesting questions, aren't they? If maintaining control over your future is vital to you, then it seems logical that you will wish to take appropriate action for a desirable exit when, and if, the time arrives. However, according to numerous studies, you probably aren't taking steps to ensure a smooth exit strategy.

It's not for lack of attention to the problem, though, because business advisors frequently push their clients to prepare for an ultimate exit. City governments quiz companies in their tax base about their plans, and the media's attention to the growing *perfect storm* of effects that unprepared businesses will have on our economic health and wealth should convince boomers to burn the midnight oil.

So, why do we have to convince you to get a move on?

Having spent the last two decades helping owners grow and prepare for succession, transition of ownership and exit, we are keenly aware that owners don't know that they need to know critical information that will help change the tide of inaction. The most powerful message we have is that there are immediate benefits to getting this preparation work underway. *You don't have to wait for the exit date before claiming more of your wealth!* In the meantime, the work of preparing your company so that it is in saleable condition will make the business more profitable.

Our philosophy guides our methodology in helping owners claim their wealth. The secret to our success is in the cracking of the code for owners regarding how their company makes and loses money. And, we don't follow the usual breadcrumb trail. We see a business as an interdependent system much like an engine, greased by the free flow of information. Employees power the engine, but the trick to high performance and profitability is the timely and effortless flow of information and knowledge throughout the company. A company functions at high performance when the leader is the mechanic, not one of the cylinders.

We are mechanics, too.

Using another analogy, we're similar to sports coaches. For instance, if players don't work on their communication strategies to signal each other, or they don't eat right, their mental game lacks sharpness. When players don't get the right cues from each other, they react in conflict. Despite all of their skills and talents, the sport suffers because of the weaknesses of the areas that are ignored. Yet pointing to any one of those areas and indicating that one is the culprit over the other, doesn't work either. It's never one person or one aspect of the whole system that is the culprit. Nonetheless, we see managers and owners repeatedly search for lone culprits, as if benching one player will make all of the other ignored (or unknown) issues disappear. And the result is a lot of angry, disappointed and sad players (and, fans!) with a frustrated coach.

A great coach, such as a great leader, owner or exit planning advisor, pays attention to mental, emotional, physical, psychological, financial, and operational concerns, as well as the interplay and interconnection among these factors.

The issues of not being saleable or profitable exist in pockets throughout the entire system. Once the system is tuned, then attention is spent noticing and fine-tuning the bumps, grinds and blocks to information flow, and educating the owner about how to become the mechanic of the company. Now, we have a high performance team ready to take on any challenge, be it the Indy 500 or attracting the exit deal of your dreams.

'Team' is the operative word for exit planning. For instance, we work with partnerships most often because partners talk to each other about their future. They are already a team, and they push each other to action in a way that single-owner companies don't experience. This is also true for larger groups of shareholders. But, invariably, every partnership grinds noisily with a host of frustrations, conflicts and unmet expectations . . . and, that's how these business teams often find us – a referral from a friend who listens to their frustrations.

The partners often know it could be different. They want their conversations to be different, but they don't know how to get past the unfinished business that has piled up over the years, and they don't know what is confounding their best intentions. Unless the solo owners are talking about what's getting in their way with a trusted source, they often don't know there are solutions and they don't realize they are creating many of their company's mechanical problems.

During our years of working with the Mergers and Acquisitions (M&A) and private sectors, we discovered that both groups struggle to understand each other, and they are frustrated when promising deals between a potential buyer and seller don't culminate with a closed transaction at the end of a long, arduous process.

We see the same, low-performance team challenges and grinding information exchange dilemmas with every project we accept. Because of our divergent backgrounds, as well as our many years of working with numerous types of varied businesses, we see and hear the same patterns repeatedly. *Why companies are not profitable. Why partners and shareholders mistrust each other. Why deals don't work out. Why companies stumble and shrink when they embark on growth strategies.*

How did we get to these realizations?

Well, Lorraine was a software entrepreneur in the '80s, long before there were many technology investors. When she noticed other business owners had the same problems she had growing and funding a company, she took what she learned into the consulting arena. She developed a methodology for growth based on identifying and rectifying profitability leaks and barriers. Lorraine also determined that leading managers and employees through the necessary changes is often the hardest business mindset adjustment for most clients to grasp.

So, she developed a set of easy-to-use tools that helped business owners become mechanics, enabling them to diagnose what wasn't working in their system and how to change their mindset *and* their ways of working with the problem. Having worked with more than 100 companies over the years, from manufacturing to clean tech, retail and professional services, Lorraine's insights and coaching approach allow the organizational machinery to work fluidly, thereby optimizing profitability.

Rob's work as a counselor and behavior specialist for youth at risk, as well as a chaplain and negotiator, provides unique skills that get at the heart of why human interactions are often mired in the muck. His talent is advising leaders, owners, military commanders and CEOs about how to get out of their own way to clean up unfinished business, so they can unleash the potential of their leadership skills, work to their strengths and trust their people. Combined with Lorraine's methodology, they built the system you are about to learn.

We have spent the last ten years working with and interviewing the intermediaries, organizations and people who facilitate the buying and selling of businesses.

In our quest to help our own clients (businesses that desire to grow) acquire other companies or prepare for their own exit, these observations emerged:

- Business owners have many erroneous belief systems about selling their companies that tend to block new information, or they consult a narrow group of people who don't have complete information. The result? They don't collect the right knowledge, so action doesn't happen.

- Business owners run operations in a way that serves their needs, which may be at cross purposes to a buyer's interests and risk profile.

- Intermediaries don't educate business owners, except when they meet face to face over a boardroom table to discuss if and how they may sell the company. The result? The owner discovers there is much work to accomplish in order to attract a buyer at the precise moment they are ready to throw in the towel.

- Business owners speak the language of operations and to-do lists; intermediaries speak the language of finance and deal making – and, buyers or their agents know what to look for to match their own deal criterion. Guess what? The owner never received the rules of the game. The result? A huge communication and timing gap.

- Intermediaries will share the criteria of what an owner must do to spruce up the company's ability to attract a buyer . . . but, owners don't get that list until it's almost too late to do anything about it. The owner is ready to sell now, not two years from now. In addition, optimizing the company's valuation (using a buyer's criterion) so that the owner can realize their expected valuation, takes time and know-how which the intermediary isn't in the business of providing. Preparing a business for sale requires making many operational, management, communication and leadership changes to get the system functioning so it's attractive to the right buyer. The result? Neither the business owner nor the intermediary knows 'how' to help each other get what the other needs or wants within the short term.

As consultants for the last twenty years, nothing is more excruciating for us than witnessing the light extinguishing in an owner's eyes who has just been approached by an intermediary or buyer (who is ready to move on to the next more lucrative deal), as they realize their company is not saleable.

Similar to agents reviewing book proposals or producers looking at scripts, the typical private equity group may look at 900 companies a year and invest in just two to five of those businesses. A strategic buyer will search their select market niche for the one or two gems they will acquire per year.

Many owners aren't considering private equity or strategic buyers for the transfer of ownership, because they envision someone closer to home taking the reins. Nonetheless, to make this transition effective, it requires an owner to gain a new perspective on the purpose of their business.

A company is in business to serve the needs of many stakeholders, ranging from customers to suppliers and employees, not just the owners. Your company needs to continue to serve its stakeholders despite your own personal plans, needs and agendas. *Never confuse what the company needs with what you, the owner, desire or need.* Trust that keeping your company's legacy thriving will also address your personal needs.

The company is going to need its next leader before you're ready to exit. Most businesses that have employees may need much greater preparation than you think.

Consider these questions:

1. Are you thinking your employees might like to buy you out?

2. Have you prepared them to be able to do that? Financially, it can take five to seven, or possibly ten years, for that kind of transaction to play out.

3. Are you thinking family members will take over one day?

4. Have you had the conversation to make sure that they want to, are ready for and have the leadership skills and financial capacity to purchase your position in an arms-length transaction?

5. Do you want your partners to buy you out? Are you able to have the kind of conversation needed to develop a comprehensive plan and structure to which all agree?

6. Do you have a general manager who can take over all of your functional jobs and knows your key clients? Will this person be able to buy your position over an extended period?

What conversations like these are you waiting to have, so you can disembark the train when you're ready?

Chances are, proactive action is not happening because you aren't aware of the immediate and long-term opportunity, so the work of preparing your business isn't high on your agenda; and, in fact, you may think it is just a functional planning exercise. Preparing yourself to lift your hands off the controls requires much deeper exploration before you, an owner, can begin to plan;

however, your conflicting emotions about the future may be blocking your action.

Nonetheless, you should know that if you prepare your company for sale now and don't wait, your company will be more profitable and much easier for you to operate than it is now. In fact, by choosing to start the work of preparation, you will be claiming your wealth long before you need to exit.

We know this is true! We see greater profitability emerge at every company with which we've worked!

If you're in the majority of business owners, you probably don't know how to start this journey or whom to talk to; it can be confusing and piece meal. Advisors focus on personal financial preparation and transferring management roles, as if that is all that's necessary to be ready to sell a business. Wealth planning may be well underway, but the formula for the rest of the equation regarding saleability is scattered among a variety of experts.

There isn't a single source of information on the entire formula for successful exits.

Until now!

Until recently, what makes a business attractive to an investor in the boardroom of a private equity or strategic buyer, is its financing partners. And, usually, these facts are not well explained until a business owner is in front of a broker hoping for a quick sale due to uncontrollable circumstances. You can well imagine that, by then, it's too late to optimize for saleability. To complicate matters, each buyer type (and lender) has varied criteria guiding their decisions.

The nature of many business owners is to keep their own counsel and push away any information that they don't need immediately. It may *seem* as if the person giving advice is trying to take control away with that information and, with that attitude, important and difficult conversations don't take place; plans don't materialize.

Economic uncertainty adds more confusion to the mix of issues, adding to the stress of owners. The hands-on role owners play in their companies leaves very little time for anything other than dealing with and reacting to daily business demands. Being tactical in the moment is far more satisfying than thinking in more abstract and strategic terms for the future. And, to top it off, there is such a steep learning curve about what to do and whom to talk to, that exit planning keeps getting pushed further down the 'to-do' list.

While preparing a company for attractiveness to a buyer is complicated, if you want the exit of your dreams and you make a commitment to get the desired result, then your company can become saleable. A commitment to learning, getting help, changing mindsets and implementing the right plan succeeds in getting the job done. And, this path to success is exactly the same journey taken to start and grow the business. The distinction between the start-up journey and the transfer of ownership journey is the critical success factor that we reveal in this book.

To the rest of the world, the need for a plan is obvious; however, there isn't much integration in the advisory world to pull together all the needed parts of the journey so they're all in one place. This book, the supporting PlayBook and available online training at www.MakeYourBusinessSaleable.com, will demystify the entire saleability process. We're bringing all of the information to you, so you can follow a useful and cohesive framework that breaks through the seemingly insurmountable barriers.

If you have a framework or a blueprint to follow regarding how to make sure your company catches the eye of an appropriate buyer, are you willing to make the necessary changes (starting today) in order to grasp that certainty?

We frequently witness some of the most excruciating moments in the history of our business lives when business owners discover the news that their company is not in saleable condition. *The silence in the room says it all.* It's devastating for a business owner to hear from brokers or mergers and acquisitions professionals that he or she needs to do a little (OK – a lot!) 'spring cleaning', and make a few changes. ARGHH! All they want to do is find a buyer – yesterday! Even if you want to, you can't make the kinds of changes a buyer seeks within a scant few months. In addition, you can't go about it in a way that will lessen the risk for the buyer.

By reading *Fast-Track Secrets for Making Your Business Saleable*, you will discover what to do, and why you can't make such changes in a big hurry during the most stressful event of your life.

Sounds like a lot to cram into your brain, doesn't it? It doesn't have to get to this point, though! Don't live with all that angst, risk and drama! Choose to learn how to prepare your company so you can claim your wealth, and then work through the steps for two-to-four years, so you get what you really want, when you want it!

Being saleable depends on many complex factors that are at the heart of this book. Your exit strategy determines the elements needed for saleability.

Think about being saleable the same way you would think about your home being saleable. It is saleable if there is a willing buyer for your home's qualities and unique characteristics. Your house has to appeal to a buyer who wants everything your house represents. Of all the potential buyers in the market at any given time, only a subset will want what your home offers. Increase the desirability factors and you increase the percentage of interested buyers.

While becoming saleable may seem like a project for the future, doing the work now has far bigger, immediate benefits in store for those of you who make the decision to become saleable.

Want to know what's possible when you prepare and implement the saleability blueprint to transition the ownership of your business?

- Employees take on more responsibility for management, sales, operations and organizational development, thereby leaving you free to lead strategy.

- The issues that plague your profitability become 'reminiscing stories' with the managers who help you fix the leaks.

- The base of customers grows, and their loyalty to your brand expands; the headaches that keep you up at night transform into solutions, making you leap out of bed in the morning.

- Opportunities to which you had to say, "No" to in the past are now well within your grasp, and people who won't consider doing business with your company now are forging new partnerships.

- Star performers in your company rise up in their careers, and they jockey for the top spots in your company.

- Strategic buyers call you to see if you have interest in selling your company, and return on your investment moves into double-digit territory (possibly for the first time).

- You look forward to relinquishing control of the business because you are moving to a more vital, purposeful future, and you're secure in the knowledge that your company will thrive under new ownership.

- You achieve the value of your business that you dream of – all of the years you invested in making the company what it is today reward you with a profitable, great place to work that delivers value for its customers and shiny returns for its owners.

How does that sound? Well, trust us – all of it happens when you focus on planning the proper exit, and you start building your two-to-four-year plan for making your company sale worthy.

When you decided to be proactive by purchasing Fast-Track Secrets for Making Your Company Saleable, you also decided to learn how it all works. Kudos to you for recognizing this crucial step!

We will share with you how to transform your business from something in which you currently survive or merely hang on to for the near future, into the ticket to maximum returns for you and all of the people who rely on your company.

There are so many benefits to reap by taking the exit plan plunge – so, why is it that statistics portray a nation of procrastinators, pushing off the discussion of how they will claim their wealth from the largest asset they have ever known? We don't get it! Or maybe we do and it's time to explain it to everyone else who is waiting for business owners to act.

Our experience tells us that the lack of preparation points to more complex issues . . . not just the fact that an exit plan isn't in place. Getting ready to sell a company can be an emotional and existential struggle, as well as a complicated, functional problem.

You can't write an exit plan if you haven't decided what's important to you!

Owners talk about exiting their companies in a negative light – rather than seeing opportunity they see endless days of boredom, adrift in a purposeless and nebulous place called retirement.   But, what if they don't wear their company identity anymore – what will they do next? How will people measure their worth if there aren't any accomplishments? What bragging rights remain?

Rather than dealing with these internal conflicting emotions, as well as the reactions of people around them, the typical owner reverts to his or her comfort zone. For owners who aren't comfortable with their own needs, *fear of the future* may play a huge role in building and implementing this plan.

Focusing on a future that doesn't include connecting to their business community and employee family anymore can feel very lonely. Not finding anything to get up and fight for in the morning can put fear in the hearts of even the toughest business leaders.

There are also other external reasons keeping the exit plan sitting on the bench. If your company suffers setbacks due to the economy, a bright future doesn't seem possible, does it? If we were in your shoes, our thoughts would turn to, "So, why bother with an exit plan? My company is too small – no one is going to buy it!" Yet, until you invest time in learning more, you won't discover what options are available to you.

Transitioning a business is more difficult when you don't recognize and work with these strong emotional currents by navigating and charting your desired future. Put your oars in the water and you'll soon master maneuvering through eddies and whirlpools through which this exit river will take you.

What if you have partners? They, too, have differing needs, time horizons and agendas regarding how they will exit from the business. The discord of opposing voices many times bars the partners from discussing the creation of an exit plan that maximizes everyone's rewards. A smart exit plan harmonizes all needs. However, partners often spend fruitless hours searching for satisfying compromises or accommodating the noisiest among shareholders.

Yes, there never seems to be enough time to do anything, but work on or in the business – which is bad news for all of us. If you want to make any changes, you have to schedule this goal in your calendar.

How many of these factors sound like you or your situation?

––––––––––––

A written plan is only part of your need as a business owner. The purpose of this book is to help you start and complete the journey of examining and learning about all of the aspects of preparing a business for sale. From the difficult personal and interpersonal issues, to the functional requirements for being attractive to a specific buyer, we'll place you on the fast track to a successful sale by teaching you what you need to know.

So. You are beginning to recognize that an exit plan involves much more than conventional wisdom suggests. Looking only at the functional dynamics or the numbers is like planning a trip to Mount Everest, buying all of the gear, and hiring the best guide without getting into physical and emotional shape. Obviously, to the armchair quarterback, this is very short sighted. *Can you imagine?* Picture yourself on Mount Everest . . . you have everything you need. The sad irony is you will come face to face with your personal limitations – your emotional and mental state – *long* before you ever get to use all of your gadgets. And it will be a big surprise when you hit *that* wall.

It may take getting external support to get you there, but if you choose to be proactive and create an exit plan, you will reap the benefits and rewards. You'll realize what you want, and you won't wait for circumstances to make the decision for you.

By building your blueprint, you will have solutions for how you will:

- Portray a vital role in your next act in life
- Stay connected to your business community
- Get up in the morning with something worthwhile for which to fight
- Continue to achieve meaningful and enriching results
- Share what matters to you with friends and family
- Recover from economic setbacks
- Work in tandem and in harmony with partners toward common goals
- Restore profitability
- Find the right exit partner that fits your business, financial and time horizon goals

- Share, and even pass on, responsibilities to managers and employees.

How does all of that sound? Good?

Then this is the book for you! We'll help you get started, not just learn about what is involved in preparing your business for sale – you will have a plan of action and starting point; you'll move forward from *thinking* about your business becoming more profitable and saleable, to *achieving* a business that is profitable and saleable. And, in the process, you'll gain a much better return on your investment!

What can be better than that?

So, get off the bench! You *don't* have to sit on the sidelines waiting for life's circumstances to pull the rug out from under you. You *don't* have to avoid the succession discussion or transition discussion with your team. You *don't* have to lie awake at night wondering how you are going to keep it all going. *All you have to do is decide to read this book, tackle the exercises, follow the quick start guide, and then share thoughts and plans with friends and family.* If you do that, then you'll take your first steps toward your dream! You'll feel remarkably unencumbered – and, when that happens, you can design the right course of action based on our recommendations. Even thinking about it, makes you feel 'lighter' already!

Every business owner can take these steps. The question is – *will you take these steps*? Are you willing to begin your learning journey in an effort to create your plan, and make the necessary changes to create your desired result?

Rob and I wrote this book because after two decades of helping business owners become better at growing their companies and preparing them for sale, we know that the biggest obstacle to getting what you really want is to stop thinking about what you don't want – then get the right help!

What do we mean by that? You might envision all of the ways that this plan won't work. After all, who could really run the business as well as the owner? The company is successful and, if anyone else steps in and takes it to a new level, does that negate the owner's success? No! Not in the least. But, for some owners, this idea is a tough mindset to relinquish.

Here's the rub. Owners get lost in the daily 'to-do list' of their operations, and they don't take the time to step out of that mindset to manage their futures effectively. They are too busy to learn how to be strategic and ready, or even to discover that they can have much more control over the entire process *if* they build a plan two-to-four years before they want to sell.

If you're like the majority of business owners,[1] an overwhelming 70% of employer business owners reported that their business was their primary source of income compared to 44% of non-employer firms. The owner of a firm with employees tends to need more complex exit planning[2] compared to a sole proprietor for the following reasons:

- There are simply more stakeholders (employees, partners, shareholders, bankers, suppliers and customers rely on your business financially and in other ways.)

- Employer firms tend to be larger, with greater scope and scale. About 25% of all American businesses are employer firms as opposed to non-employer firms or sole proprietorships.

- Employer business owners tend to be more financially dependent on their businesses and, therefore, they identify personally with its success.

---

[1] 2002 Census Bureau's Characteristics of Business Owners (CBO) Survey

[2] Leonetti, John. "Business Exit Strategy Planning: A Growth Niche"
http://www.pinnacleequitysolutions.com/public/107print.cfm

- Businesses with employees generate 96% - 97% of all sales receipts. In 2002, the average employer firm generated $1.7 million in sales receipts, while the average sole proprietor made just under $44,000.

But preparing your company for sale is not just your personal concern. What's the problem if some owners might not take the initiative to build and execute a plan? There is a more profound issue at stake regarding the lack of time and effort being put into preparing a business for transition of ownership.

Of the total 20.5 million business owner respondents to the 2002 Census Bureau COB Survey, 5.6 million are owners of employer firms. We know that 80% of all business owners are now over the age of fifty; and, if we apply this percentage to the number of employer firms, there are 3.2 million business owners in need of immediate exit planning. Without that planning, many of these 3.2 million companies are not saleable in their current condition. Any sizeable percentage of this group not able to sell or transition ownership will have a substantial effect on our economy, given that these businesses earn 96% of all dollar receipts of the 50% of businesses that power the economy.

Should a majority of owners be forced into circumstances that are between a rock and a hard place, and having to wind down or hand over a business that could have generated a lot more for lack of advanced planning, the effect on every age group will be pronounced.

From 2009, roughly 750,000 businesses, per year, need to transition their ownership over the next ten to fifteen years. Prior to the aging of boomers, there was a fraction of owners selling. Burgeoning supplies of businesses for sale will put downward pressure on company valuations, and when the supply of companies for sale surges, buyers can afford to be very picky about what they want to acquire.

The unprepared business owners will have few choices if they leave their futures to circumstances such as disease, divorce, uncontrollable variables or death that demand the sale or liquidation of assets. In addition, this situation has even more profound impacts that may affect entire towns, industries and people.

If the goal of becoming saleable is not impetus enough for you to start taking action this year, think about these facts: 3.2 million businesses generate most of the economic returns that power our local communities. Look around your town. Think of the businesses you know, your suppliers, competitors, value chain, members of your industry association and community or business clubs. How gray are they[3]?

If the company owners in your network have not developed a plan to claim their wealth, what happens to the future of those businesses? Companies from which you buy materials may close, forcing you to look elsewhere, retool, and absorb the costs of such changes. When local government loses an employer, its tax base shrinks, thereby adding to losses in property tax revenue from the real estate bubble bursting.

As a community faces this contraction in economic health, the collective mood declines, affecting civility that places a burden on social services. This domino effect increases when a city, town or area has numerous businesses, all in limbo, due to the graying of our economic engines.

This tidal surge will also affect associations. What will happen to your industry? As the wealth of experience and knowledge wanes, the connections that disperse practical wisdom and support shared best practices erode.

---

[3] Pletz, John. The Graying of Chicago *Crane's Business* http://www.chicagobusiness.com/article/20110205/ISSUE01/302059982/crains-special-report-the-graying-of-chicago#axzz1DyCh44Za February 7, 2011

The choices owners make and the speed with which they begin to implement the changes to become saleable will have a profound effect on all of us. We wrote this book to spur action, to engage business owners across the country to want more from their next step in life, and to show them how to get started. *Preparing your company for sale is the right thing to do for so many more reasons than you might ever have imagined!*

Which boat do you want your company to be sitting in as this tidal surge happens? To be in demand by buyers or part of the over-supply? To ensure your legacy thrives or to watch as the value of your assets erodes, the longer you wait to prepare your exit plan? To be part of the solution that revitalizes your community or one that adds to the domino effect it faces?

The prepared business owners engaged in implementing a well thought out saleability plan will be able to choose when, how much and who acquires their assets; and, they will contribute vital stability to stakeholders.

By reading this book and setting out blocks of time to follow the plan you will create, you will do far more than give your family a secure financial future. You will leave a legacy that reverberates and ripples across the country for the good of all.

HOW SALEABLE IS YOUR BUSINESS?

"Everything you now do is something you have chosen to do. Some people don't want to believe that. But if you're over age twenty-one, your life is what you're making of it. To change your life, you need to change your priorities."

John C. Maxwell[4]

Take the guesswork out of your future! Claim your wealth! Learn how to prepare your company, so you can exit when you want and for the amount you desire.

---

[4] Maxwell, John C. "Today Matters: Twelve Daily Practices to Guarantee Tomorrow's Success". *Center Street Publishing, New York, NY* 2004

Section I
Orientation

In this section, you will learn:

- What is involved in an exit
- The challenges involved in being able to sell a business
- The two critical questions that need answering in order to start building an exit plan
- How to use this book and get the most out of it

Chapter 1
Is Peter's Business Saleable?

It's a bright sunny day, and Peter is having lunch with an advisor. They are sitting on the patio of his golf club talking about what Peter will be able to do once he's lightened his workload. He runs his hands through still thick salt and pepper hair, his hands and words painting a picture in a voice filled with enthusiasm. His back won't bother him then. He'll teach his grandson how to fish. Maybe even take one of those volunteer vacations his wife tells him about. And be done dealing with the good, the bad and the frustration of owning a company with partners. He laughs.

The advisor asks Peter when he might be able to 'lighten his workload'. Will he hire someone to run the company? Or, does that day come only once he's sold the company?

Peter shifts in his chair and squints as if the sun is now too bright. He focuses on the table where his buzzing Blackberry is parked next to the remnants of his lunch. He pushes his sunglasses over his eyes. Lightening his load won't be possible until the company is sold. His voice returns to its former serious clip, and he leans back in his chair as a sigh escapes.

The advisor asks when Peter thinks he will be able to do that.

The cloud appears.

Peter considers for a long moment and then he offers a story. A friend who owns a distribution business just had a pretty good offer put on the table. It came unexpectedly from a big company

23

back east, and he's thinking he should take it. "I would," he says. "Of course he doesn't have partners. Different kind of business, too." Another sigh. "What do we have to do to get into the same position? Are there buyers for a technical consulting firm? Is it even possible to think we could sell?"

The questions are delivered rapid fire and then stop.

"Can we get it done this year?" His voice is hopeful and hesitant. "For around $20 million perhaps?"

The advisor hears this question a lot. "Is that number close to what it's actually worth, Peter? There are always buyers for good businesses, but every business is in a unique situation. And the number? That depends on whether you've made it attractive to the kind of buyers that want technical consulting firms in a growing market niche. Those are some of the things that determine when you'll be ready to sell it."

The advisor notices the answer provided is not what Peter is expecting.

"And, would you all agree on that value? How attached are your partners to that number? Most important, it depends on whether the company is actually in saleable condition. Is it?"

Peter thinks for a while. "What does saleable mean? How do I find out find out if PSWA is saleable before I get my partners' hopes up?"

Coming to Terms

It used to be that when an owner decided it was finally time to sell, all it took was a few calls and a transaction with a buyer often materialized. Forty or fifty years ago, entrepreneurs were rare. Companies kept growing; they weren't sold. However, boomers changed all that, and owners now have the freedom of choice regarding a company's future: to grow, to acquire other companies, or to sell to larger companies, employees, financiers, new partners or individuals. But with more freedom of options, comes complexities and difficult decisions. Some of these options require dedicated focus to a path of action in order to achieve the desired result.

Today's business owner faces a convergence of events. The market for private transactions has evolved, buyers have become more sophisticated and, therefore, more discerning; scrutiny of deals is more intense, and while there are many more buyers of private companies in the market, you may think that finding the right match between buyer and seller should be easier.

Not so much.

There is, however, a larger imbalance that may affect the ability of business owners to claim their wealth. The supply of owners wanting to sell is greater than demand. Buyers and deal financiers are looking for specific key performance indicators to tell them what is worth investment.

The emerging conclusion is that only those businesses of interest to buyers and those that qualify for transition financing or buy-outs will find an exit partner.

To qualify means to be saleable.

What of the rest?

According to the Small Business Administration (SBA), boomers entering what used to be called 'retirement age', own 50% of all businesses (approximately 10,000,000). Of that 10,000,000, 3,200,000 have employees such as Peter and his partner. The owners of these companies are privately wondering if their future dreams are even possible. And maybe the old idea of retirement should be thrown out in favor of living a vibrant life on your own terms – which can be done, if you have the freedom to use the money from claiming your wealth. Many boomers have pushed the date too far into the future, and their uncertainty about their own interests affects the company's saleability. *Let's be clear, preparing your company to become saleable offers you the freedom to make all sorts of decisions.* Indecision stalls any thinking, planning or action. And, like anything when we don't make a decision, circumstance takes over and makes the decisions for us. Without decisive, immediate action, and commitment to focus, these owners will have to face the fact that the biggest asset they invested in for years will not deliver expected returns for a good post-exit lifestyle.

They will end up working longer.

Preparing your company for sale is a social, economic and ethical responsibility, and not just your personal concern. What happens if some owners might not take the initiative to build and execute a plan? There is a more profound issue at stake regarding the lack of time and effort put into preparing a business for transition of ownership.

If circumstances force a majority of owners into 'between a rock and a hard place', having to wind down or hand over a business that could have generated more income, but didn't because of a lack of advanced planning, they will have a pronounced effect on every age group.

Since 2009, roughly 750,000 businesses, per year, need to transition their ownership over the next ten to fifteen years. Prior to the aging of boomers, only a fraction of all owners was selling. A burgeoning supply of businesses for sale will put downward pressure on company valuations and, when the supply of companies for sale surges, buyers can afford to be very finicky about which companies they wish to acquire. The early bird will get the worm!

The unprepared and late-to-the-party business owners will have few choices if they leave their future to circumstances such as disease, divorce, uncontrollable variables or death. Everyday life may demand the sale or liquidation of assets, and these situations have even more profound impacts on entire towns, industries and people.

If the company owners in your network have not developed a plan to claim their wealth, what happens to the future of those businesses? Companies from which you buy materials may close, thereby forcing you to look elsewhere, retool and absorb the costs of such changes. When local government loses an employer, their tax base shrinks, which is on top of losses in property tax revenue from the burst of the real estate bubble.

As a community faces this contraction in economic health, the collective mood declines and affects civility, which places a burden on social services. This domino effect increases when a city, town or area has numerous businesses in limbo, due to the graying of our economic engines.

This tidal surge will also affect associations. What will happen to your industry? As the wealth of experience and knowledge declines and decreases, the connections that disperse practical wisdom and support shared-best practices, erodes. The pace of innovation and productivity declines.

The choices owners make and the speed with which they begin to implement the changes to become saleable, will have a profound effect on all of us. We wrote this book to spur action, to engage business owners across the country to want more from their next step in life, and to show them how to get started.

The prepared business owner engaged in implementing a well thought out saleability plan will be able to choose when, how much and who acquires their assets, as well as contribute vital stability to stakeholders.

There is a lot of good news for the early bird!

Buyers seek out companies that have done the work to become saleable! We know owners who were paid a premium, much more than they thought possible, just because they had done their homework and become the acquirer's ideal target. What would a few more million mean to you and your family?

According to Capital IQ[5], professional buyers complete 12,000 deals per year (other companies making acquisitions and private equity investors). Many more companies are bought and sold off the radar of these statistics by professionals 'buying a job', by employees or managers buying control over their future, by immigrants buying a stake in their new country, by business partners buying each other out or through families' ceding the day-to-day operation to the next generation.

Not all businesses will find a solution that helps owners claim their wealth. Some may be working long past typical retirement age and some may just wind it down, having paid themselves a handsome wage over the years. However, many owners may let the business lapse due to inaction and lack of reflection, without having learned that other options might have been possible if only they had started working on a plan earlier – before market forces, irrelevancy, tiredness, divorce, disease or death come to call.

Despite these statistics, there are multiple ways to find an exit. The secret is to learn what it takes to position your company, create a plan and stay the course to achieve it.

To infiltrate the set of owners that will be able to sell, you must ask and answer two interrelated questions:

---

[5] Capital IQ "Market Observations: High-level perspectives of public equity, credit markets, private capital M&A and more" *McGraw-Hill Companies, Inc.* January 2011

Exploration Exercise #1
Taking Stock

1. How much money do you want to have when you exit?

2. What legacy do you want to leave behind for your employees, customers and community stakeholders, so that they also have a bright future?

Gaining clarity about how you want to make this exit is a step that most business owners misunderstand, don't adequately plan for and don't realize there is much more to this journey than picking a successor, date and exit number.

The amount you want at your exit may be enough to cover your needs. But, is it, realistically, an amount a buyer will pay for the right to the company's future earnings? By reconciling well in advance of the time you want to sell, the discrepancy between what you want for the company and what a buyer might pay, you will give yourself adequate time to optimize and position your company to be attractive for sale and, most important, become worth the amount you desire.

We call this closing the gap.

Secondly, by considering this reconciliation in value, you open the door to solidify your legacy and leave a bright future for those stakeholders you are leaving behind.

Looking at the situation in another way, if you can't sell the company when you want and for the amount you desire, what happens to your future, the business and its stakeholders?

Once you have thought about and answered these two questions, you will be in a better position to come to terms with the next hurdle on the way to becoming saleable.

Buyers we have interviewed say the number one reason why deals don't come together is that the owner gets in the way.

Buyers cannot acquire a company when:

- The owner is still running the company or playing a functional role, unless they have clear objectives to become part of and work for the new owner's management team.

- The management team doesn't have the record of accomplishment to show they are able to plan and implement the forecast expectations without the owner at the helm.

Unless you want to continue working for the new owner, which may happen for at least a few months or years, part of your preparation work must be to replace yourself. You may need this step sooner than you think, because preparing a company to be saleable will take strong leadership, purposeful action and an investment of time. Your functional role must soon be delegated.

The next essential element in the plan for becoming saleable is to select the most appropriate type of buyer two-to-four years before your desired exit date. Then you can set goals to remodel or optimize the company, so that it is attractive to those specific buyers.

If you have a family-owned business, there may be three additional elements that you will want to consider. You have built a company that should remain a going concern, so that it continues to provide value to your customers; and, therefore, it is a viable place to work for employees and it continues to provide a return for your family. If leaving this kind of legacy is important to you, then you may also need to consider these concerns in your exit plan:

- Gifting your company to an interested family member in order to keep it in the family proves to be a major contributor to a company's decline.[6]

---

[6] Deans, Thomas William. "Every Family's Business" *Detente Financial Press Orangeville, ON* 2008

- Selling the company to family members at fair market value will ensure the buyer continues to build on top of your work. Treat the deal as an arms' length transaction to eliminate the possibility of moral hazard. People fight for that in which they are invested.

Leaving your company in good hands is important to its future ability to deliver returns. Expect that the family member who buys the company should also have the skills needed to lead the company to the growth expectations you have set in order to justify the valuation you desire.

Think and Act Ahead of the Pack

Regardless of whether the company is a partnership, family-owned or solely owned, those business owners who optimize the company to close the value gap and focus on a particular type of buyer, can increase their chances of finding a willing buyer and closing a deal. The day to start this work is two-to-four years before you want to sell.

To get started on this two-to-four-year process, it helps to complete four critical steps to prepare yourself, your company and its future, so that it gives the return a buyer wants and the exit value you're seeking. In summary, your four steps to becoming a 'saleable company' are:

- ✓ Handle Reality
- ✓ Hone Decisions and Goals
- ✓ Hunt the Right Acquirer
- ✓ Helm Change

Steps 2 and 3 may need to be done concurrently – Steps 1 and 4, independently, and in that order.

You may have a little or a lot of work to do in order to stand out from your competitors in this buyer's market. In this book, we explain the work involved in each element of this framework, so you can use it as a study guide and a planning tool. In addition, you'll use it as a roadmap to help you get to your desired result – a profitable company that is attractive to the right buyer, and who is willing to buy at a price and time that works for you and your stakeholders.

The High Price of Following Conventional Wisdom

Have you honed your personal and corporate goals? Decided what's in your future and your company's future? No matter what the economic climate, you and your employees have many options that you might not be aware of for becoming more profitable and eventually selling your company. Rest assured, investors are buying and profitability is achievable even in a slow growth to flat economy. What's the secret that many owners are missing? *You may need to suspend or let go of ideas you thought were conventional wisdom about what it takes to make a business interesting to a buyer, selling a business and learning more about how you can achieve profitability.*

The number-one secret is to perform the work to become more profitable and operationally optimized with a great management team, well in advance of the date you want to sell. Then, your firm is worth what your ideal buyer agrees it is worth. As a result, the probability of acquiring financing for your desired exit path improves.

Remember: the work you put into becoming saleable is what will improve company profits long before a sale. What is good for buyers and investors is good for you.

As an owner, you are also an investor, so learning to think like an investor is the key to understanding the concept of saleability that may coincide with helping you see how to be more profitable. What's more, better profitability is possible even if revenues are not growing, and even if you have already taken all the cost control measures you need.

'Succession planning' is the term many advisors use to encourage owners to plan for the day they sell their company. The public discourse on succession planning is often incomplete, and current definitions are missing some key success criteria.

There is Much More to Becoming Saleable than Just Succession Planning

You may have heard that succession planning is the act of hiring your replacement or transferring your knowledge and key relationships to managers in your company, as well as ensuring your estate is optimized for tax sheltering. However, this narrow definition assumes you have people in place to take over because they are capable and effective at leading and managing. Nonetheless, is this singular act going to ensure your company is saleable?

Unfortunately not. And, this is a gaping hole in the current literature and advice available to business owners today. Simply pursuing a succession plan is a poor substitute for intentionally driving your business toward the exit result you desire.

The graphic on the next page, identifies each stage of a company:

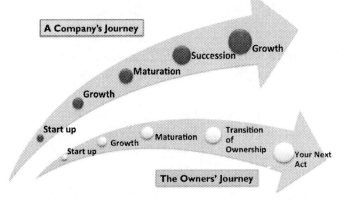

Fig. 1

Think of preparing your business to become saleable as the next logical step in your company's life. There are two separate trajectories here. For your company, there is the start up phase, the growth phase, maturation and succession phase; and, then, the next growth phase with the new owner. For you, the current owner, your paths align until it's time for you to move on to your next act in life, but your company keeps going.

Becoming saleable involves much more than selecting a replacement for you. The blueprint outlined here will prepare your company and you, personally, *before* you start succession planning. Hiring your successor is one of the last items on the list. To be able to sell means you must hunt and attract a willing investor or buyer. A buyer will look at businesses to acquire with a different set of criteria than you use to view your company.

What action you take over the next two-to-four years will influence whether or not you will be able to sell with your legacy intact; and, for the money you need to take care of your future. Some or all of the factors of saleability may apply to your industry.

The Six Factors of Saleability:

1. The business has a growth plan, so that the future owner can clearly predict what returns are available.

2. Like a finely tuned engine, all internal parts, processes and systems work in support of that growth plan.

3. The people who lead the growth plan have demonstrated they can align people, resources and actions that achieve results.

4. Profitability is predictable, and the elements that affect or form barriers to profitability are well understood, monitored and managed.

5. The growth opportunity is in a stable, growing or hot industry, or geographic area that requires more complete solutions rather than commodity and price-driven products.

6. The company has a secret sauce way of working, deep knowledge or unique intellectual property that is causing growing demand and interest in the brand.

Reality dictates there are many questions you need to investigate to engage the exit ignition engine. Armed with the truth of your situation, you can determine which road to take next in order to get to your destination. By tackling two specific issues first and coming to terms with your current state, you buy yourself enough time to optimize your operation so the company converts to a saleable condition. Using this book, you will be able to gain clarity regarding the following two questions:

- Is your firm, in its current state, desirable to a prospective buyer?

- Are you ready and able to improve profitability to hunt and attract the ideal buyer by closing the gap between the company's worth and the amount you want when you walk away?

You may not be able to answer these questions until you finish the book and do the suggested exercises. Before you start any journey, you have to know the lay of the land around where you are starting. How saleable is your company? Let's find out.

Chapter 1 Summary
How to Use This Book

We designed this book as a roadmap for your two-to-four year journey. There are four stages to the journey:

- Handle Reality
- Hone Goals and Decisions
- Hunt the Right Acquirer
- Helm Change

You will want to familiarize yourself with the work involved in all of these steps, and then begin working through the recommendations for action. There are exercises and checklists for each stage that you can complete in the accompanying PlayBook. Once you have finished working through the exercises, you should be well informed enough to draw your conclusions and to start to take appropriate actions to handle, hone, hunt and helm your journey to the exit of your dreams. Use the PlayBook to capture your responses to the exercises, and add notes and ideas to help shape your action plan. Let it serve as a repository of your thoughts, feelings, plan ideas and commitments as you start your journey toward the exit of your dreams. Your PlayBook becomes your action blueprint.

Your company may be saleable. Taking the time to learn what 'being saleable' means can help you determine how you can plan and achieve an exit that meets your needs and goals. It will also provide the opportunity to discover a bright future for the great company you have worked so hard to build once you leave.

Section II
Saleability Blueprint Basics

"Social scientists have determined that we accept inner responsibility for a behavior when we think we have chosen to perform it in the absence of strong outside pressures. A large reward is one such external pressure. It may get us to perform a certain action, but won't get us to accept inner responsibility for the act. Consequently, we won't feel committed to it. The same is true of a strong threat; it may motivate immediate compliance, but it is unlikely to produce long-term commitment."

Robert Cialdini[7]

In this section, you will learn about:

- How prepared your company is for sale.

- What is involved in improving your company's readiness for sale, so that you increase the probability of attracting a buyer.

- How to think about what it means to prepare for sale and have a company that is saleable.

- Building your own preparation checklist.

---

[7] Cialdini, Robert. "Influence" *HarperCollins Publishers Inc*. New York, NY 1984

Chapter 2
What is Your State of Readiness?

"A dream you dream alone is only a dream. A dream you dream together is reality."

John Lennon[8]

What you will learn about in this chapter:

- The first step in preparing your company for sale is to understand its current readiness.

- What is involved in a preparation checklist.

- How to improve your own readiness and that of the company's.

Handling reality means getting comfortable with the good, the bad and the ugly. It means laying down the blinders that might have stopped you from seeing your situation and your company's standing from a buyer or lender's perspective. It may mean changing your mindset and dealing with emotions or facts you typically push away. Certainly, it will require that you focus on what you want to do after your company is acquired. You will be far more motivated to do the work necessary if you are committed to a future plan. Or, as Cialdini notes in the quote, "To achieve

---

[8] John Winston Ono Lennon, 9 October, 1940 – 8 December, 1980, English musician and singer-songwriter, founding member of the Beatles

what you really want requires you take inner personal responsibility for the necessary work."

To be adequately prepared to sell your business for what you hope it is worth, may mean making some critical changes. However, you can't change what you can't yet see clearly. This is the one fact that should grab your attention!

Accept that you don't know how to do this work yet. Accept how making changes in one area won't be enough to offset another. Get curious about everything! Make this your mantra: "What am I missing that will help me to understand this situation **before** *I decide to act?"*

You may learn something about your company, or yourself, on the exploration journey that disagrees with your perception or opinion. Shout, "Eureka!" This is the moment to set aside any pre-conceived ideas about your company and see it from a new perspective. Your current mindset raised the business to its current success; however, it won't get you to the exit of your dreams. Changing your mindset and learning more about how you get in your own way is the first order of business on your saleability journey.

At first, what you learn might make you set aside this book and the whole idea of preparation. While this learning process might make you feel uncomfortable, remember why you are doing this preparation work. You want a good financial return for your years as a business, and your employees need to know there is a future with your company. As they watch the years tick by, they know some kind of exit, even if it isn't retirement, is on your horizon.

Your suppliers and customers need certainty or they will go elsewhere. The more uncertainty you generate with your inaction, the more risk you introduce into the business. Increased risk decreases investor and lender perception of value.

So trust that by getting comfortable with the uncomfortable, you enrich this stage of the preparation process by allowing room for this new information. Think of this stage of your life as the beginning of your next act. At the beginning of any new endeavor, one must make room for new information, new learning, new feelings and new perspectives. To learn a new sport or subject, we all go through the awkward phase of discovering how to relate to the actions we have yet to learn. We can't do that if we keep comparing our performance to activities in which we are already accomplished. Suspending judgement will make the learning journey easier and more enriching. Adults often hate to look or feel incompetent when learning something new; but, to get to that wonderful feeling of competence and capability again, we all have to be willing to scale the learning curve.

There are no guarantees in life. You can't control outcomes or other people. You activate the only real power you have by the choices you make based on the new information you learn. New information comes from this book, your own interests and your feelings – running the gamut from excitement to fear of the unknown.

Decide you want to handle reality. Look at the list of statements below to clarify where your company stands today, so you understand what is needed to reach your goal to help your company become saleable.

Exploration Exercise #2
Developing Your Preparation Checklist

We designed this exercise to help you understand your company's current state of readiness and, later, we will look at your personal state of readiness. From your responses, you will be able to see what conditions might need attention. Then you will have a preparation checklist that serves as a high-level blueprint for the changes you will want to make in order to be saleable.

You may find it useful to start a notebook dedicated to your blueprint, so you have your exit planning notes and action ideas in one location. We're including a PlayBook with all of the exercises included, so you can build on it to use for your notes; it's handy to record the answers to all Exploration Exercises in your PlayBook.

Check all of the boxes that best describe your current situation, regardless of whether you have a partnership, single ownership or family-owned business:

☐ The company has been satisfactorily profitable for your industry for the last few years, and it is now.

☐ You know what the company is worth today, and you are happy with that amount.

☐ The company is worth enough to fund your exit plans or next act (including any other investments you have).

> Your company might be in saleable condition, but not worth what you had hoped it would be in order to fund your retirement.

☐ You (and other owners) have set an exit date, you know what you will do post-sale and you are excited about the prospects.

☐ You have taken the time to become informed from many sources about what it takes to sell a company, as well as all the steps involved.

☐ You have made operational improvements that have resulted in better profitability.

☐ You and other owners, who are leaving the company once it is sold, do not have a functional day-to-day role in the company (or, you are already working toward this state.) You have a trained and qualified management team (or, second in command that is not a shareholder or interested in retiring) with clear roles, responsibility and authority that leads operations.

☐ You have a strategic plan, goals and metrics that your managers implement and you are achieving your growth goals.

☐ You have identified a specific type of buyer that will be a likely candidate to buy your business.

☐ You are working toward making it attractive to this buyer.

☐ If family owned, you have agreed that the best course of action is not to gift the business, but to let those family members who want an ownership stake raise their own funds to buy into the company.

How to Interpret the Preparation Checklist

Total up the number of boxes checked. The more you have checked, the closer you are to improving your chances of being able to sell your company.

Less than ten boxes checked? You will want to complete the Mindset exercise on page 195 and discover where your thinking and/or strategies may need to be adjusted.

How to Improve Readiness

The following list is your blueprint and your learning roadmap. The boxes you did not check become the things you will want to learn more about, and each element will need an action plan, which means how your company operates and how you lead it may need to change. By learning more about the kinds of changes that will allow you to say "Yes" to all ten statements (or, eleven statements if you have a family owned business), you will be able to set up a game plan to improve or make the necessary adjustments for each element.

1. If the company is NOT profitable now: You will want to discover more about how the company makes money and loses money, as well as makes changes to optimize operations to maximize returns. This is possible even if sales have slowed and you've cut back to the bone on expenses. Suggested Resource: Blueprint Step 1 – Handle Reality and Step 4 - Helm the Transition. Read *The 1% Difference: Small Change Big Impact* by Murray Lyons and Kelly Lyons, and *The Secrets of the 1% Difference* webinar available at www.EndeavorIQ.com.

2. If you know the valuation of your company today and you are UNhappy with that amount, you may want to explore how different types of buyers assess the value of a company. By standing in the shoes of various types of buyers, you learn how to perceive value in a way that might be quite different from your own perceptions. By working on implementing changes that improve company value and reduce buyer risk, you will make the business more attractive to a type of buyer you may not have considered before and, most likely, it will become more profitable for you, too.

3. If the company is NOT worth enough to fund all owners' post exit plans, *and* if your current valuation does not match your goals, there is a lot you can do to increase the valuation by following the blueprint for helming the business to improve operational readiness. You may need to make other investments in order to achieve an owner's exit goals. Working with a financial planner who can design a workable plan is important for all owners who view their company as their biggest and sometimes only asset. *Suggested resources: Blueprint Step 1 – Handle Reality and Step 4 – Helm the Transition. Wealth management advisors and DVDs on profitability strategies available at* www.EndeavorIQ.com *and* www.MakeYourBusinessSaleable.com.

4. If you (and other owners) have NOT set an exit date and DON'T know what you will do post-sale, and you are NOT particularly excited about the prospects, *letting go of your*

company emotionally is essential to being ready to sell. It can sometimes be uncomfortable or difficult to envision what you will do when you aren't at the helm anymore. Investigating options helps engage your curiosity and interest in designing a new lifestyle for yourself. Making the transition from an owner responsible for many to an individual only responsible for yourself and your next act is much easier when you have a destination you are looking forward to. *Suggested Resource: Blueprint Step 2 – Hone Goals. The Art of Reinvention*

www.artistryofreinvention.com.

5. If you have NOT taken the time to become informed from many sources about what it takes to sell a company, as well as all of the steps involved, now is the time! Knowledge about what to do, when and how is fragmented across many different professionals. It can make navigating an often-complicated process so much more confusing, which is why we've prepared this book to serve as a guide, so you know whom to consult for each part of the puzzle and get the advice you need to proceed.

6. If you have made operational improvements that have NOT resulted in better profitability, you may need an independent third party to look under the hood and help you spot the issues that are affecting your profit engine. Often, the problems are systemic and require a broader approach to get all parts operating efficiently. Acquirers look for healthy profitability in which to invest, as well as certainty about future cash flow. Working with an advisor helps you learn to find and fix profitability leaks and make the right changes across the organization.

> Your company might be in saleable condition, but not worth what you had hoped it would be in order to fund your retirement.

7. If you and other owners STILL have functional day-to-day roles in the company and you DON'T have a trained and qualified management team that leads operations, you can't sell a company that is still dependent on its owner(s), unless the owner wants to work for the acquirer post acquisition. Depending on the type of buyer desired, the owner may participate in the transition by coaching the new owners in operations and teaching them how to build relationships with important stakeholders. But the day-to-day operations should be reliant on the manager or management team, not the owner to be in saleable condition. Making these kinds of leadership and management transitions is a learning journey.

8. If you DON'T have a strategic plan, goals and metrics that all managers implement and are achieving your growth goals, investors, lenders and buyers can't assess what isn't measured. What they can't see translates as a risk in the deal, which lowers the valuation and their interest in acquisition. For your own sake and for investors, start to set metrics. Profitable companies work in alignment toward common goals and performance metrics. You will want to set and implement strategic goals and hold managers accountable for achieving them. Watching a dashboard that shows progress to goals can unite employees to do even more to make your company successful.

9. If you have NOT identified a specific type of buyer who will be a likely candidate to buy your business, remember that strategic and financial buyers often follow the companies they want to acquire several years before they show interest. There are many ways to get on their radar! There are several other types of buyers who may be a better fit for the size and type of your business. You will get to know how each buyer type thinks, and which type that may be the best fit for your company, so you increase your chances of finding a buyer.

As you are fine tuning the company and getting to know their interests, set goals for the kinds of key performance indicators they're seeking. Or, if you intend to sell to employees, managers, family or bring in new partners to buy you out, realize that the financial strategies that enable wealth transfer can take considerable time to set up. Your work at becoming efficient in cash management, as well as pursuing cash rich strategies, will be crucial to fulfill the buyout plan.

10. If you are NOT working toward making your business attractive to this buyer, learn what type of companies your ideal buyer seeks, and why, and ensure that your company models their critical criteria or characteristics.

Do a search of public companies in your industry on Yahoo Finance to see which are buying companies such as yours. Study news releases to gain an understanding of what aspects of the company made it attractive enough to acquire.

11. If family owned, and you have NOT agreed that the best course of action is to let those family members who want an ownership stake raise their own funds to buy into the company and, if none qualify, prepare to sell to another type of buyer. Statistics show that a business given to family members rather than by their earning their stake, rarely survives into the third generation. If preserving the wealth and keeping the company operating for employees and stakeholders is important, plan this transition accordingly. *Suggested Resource: Blueprint Step 1 – Handle Reality and Step 2 – Hone Goals.*

You may want to meet with a trained family business mediator if you think this could be a tough discussion. Then, together, you can discuss this topic so your family can understand the issues. A mediator can facilitate reactions and concerns, so that you emerge with a workable plan that blends all family members' interests. Then, work with a family intermediary to build an arm's length transaction strategy.

Now that you have a context for this new information, we will delve into each element of your four-step blueprint in the following chapters.

As you may be starting to realize, there can be a lot of work to do to be profitable *and* saleable to the right buyer, which is why it can take a minimum of two-to-four years. Implementing change is what is required. If you have a longer time horizon, you are in a much better position to make the improvements that might be needed to get the company valuation close to your desired sale price. In either case, your firm can enjoy the benefits of reduced risk and greater profitability from now on.

The True Cost of Waiting

So, now you have a much better idea of your company's current state of readiness for sale. Such a revelation may be overwhelming, and you may feel like setting the whole idea of making changes to be saleable aside. Your emotions may push you to distract yourself with 'other more important things'. Instead, take the results from the Exploration Exercises you will find throughout this book, and share the questions and your answers with your spouse, best friend or trusted advisor. Discussing current circumstances with others can often help people move forward, so that inertia doesn't assert itself.

In fact, if you find yourself yawning through this part, losing interest, finding all the reasons why you shouldn't bother with it, feeling the urge to move on to something else, or even finding yourself inexplicably angry at someone else after working on this exercise, you have just discovered how you choose to push away your fear.

Fear is a very important emotion. Pay attention to it and don't ignore it. Feel overjoyed when you finally decide to accept that even *you* experience fear. Why? When you listen to what fear has to say, you uncover important needs, interests and issues that need attention. Then, you can do something about managing those needs – but, only if you listen. Ignore your fear and it escalates to increased inaction, apathy, frustration, outbursts and a stasis position.

In our experience, men have the greatest trouble acknowledging they feel anything remotely resembling fear. Our society has hard wired it into men that it's not okay to display fear; and, many men become good at denying that it even exists in them.

Society has taught men that showing or even having emotions is a sign of weakness. Actually, the reverse is true. Everyone else can see someone whom either consciously or subconsciously declares they don't experience fear. Many of us, however, see it in others, but deny it in ourselves. Funny how we all play that game. Face the fear dragon and make friends with it. Having a dragon on your side is much better than being at the mercy of the dragon.

Don't wait to do this exercise! Taking the time now to really see what's going on under the hood lets you effectively deal with circumstances beyond your control, such as the state of the economy or the changing marketplace. By having time to make the right choices now, you stay in control and you will end that feeling of powerlessness and uncertainty that comes with being forced into making decisions when pressed for time.

Taking time to make informed decisions is a win/win situation for you and your family, the firm, your employees, your customers, the community your company serves and your lenders/ bankers and investors. But, even more important, you will be working to optimize your company for your own benefit so that you, as an investor, realize better returns. It's important to remind yourself in times of uncertainty why you are taking these steps. More time helps you know where to look for leaks and create a blueprint for how to fix any problems.

Your legacy is much wider than you may think. Remember that being proactive now will help the communities in which you do business remain economically healthy.

The most important component in starting all of this work is assessing your mindset. Concerning all acts of change, what gets in the way or helps you dig and find gold, is the mindset you bring to the tasks. Most business owners operate with a single mindset that works well for daily operations. However, you are entering a new stage in your business life, and you may need to change or rethink your mindset to facilitate moving through this stage.

Will your current mindset get you to your desired result?

Chapter 2 Summary

There are four steps to being prepared for sale: Handle, Hone, Hunt and Helm. The Preparation Checklist tells you where you stand on your journey to having a company that is attractive for sale.

Because of what you learned about how prepared you are to sell, are you ready to learn more, or do you want to throw in the towel? People often feel defeated by the results of this Exploration Exercise because they don't yet understand what is involved in making the suggested changes.

It may feel like you're facing that climb up Mount Everest. Remember when you first started or bought the business? What you didn't know then about the work involved and how all the parts would come together may feel similar to your current situation. You succeeded then! You will succeed now, too, putting one foot in front of the other and working with beneficial guidelines. You built your company with a dream in mind. Now get ready to sell your company with a new dream in mind! Choose to be one of the select owners who leads the company through a successful acquisition. Then your legacy survives, and it is positioned to thrive with its new owners. It remains a great place to work, a vital contributor to the economy and to customers. Plus, you get the exit of your dreams!

Section III
Step One: Handle Reality

"All truths are easy to understand once they are discovered; the point is to discover them."

- Galileo Galilei

In this section, you will learn:

- The actual work involved in optimizing a business
- How to avoid the barriers that can block optimization and exit
- How to assess the potential value of your firm
- How buyers assess a potential acquisition
- A buyer's perception of risk

Chapter 3
The Action Blueprint

"Happiness is really just about four things: perceived control, perceived progress, connectedness (number and depth of your relationships) and vision/meaning (being part of something bigger than yourself).

Tony Hsieh, CEO of Zappos[9]

What you will learn in this chapter:

- Understand how the blueprint works and what is involved in each step.

- Learn more about what selling your company means to you and about how the company's current state affects your state of readiness to sell.

- Determine if you are Aware, Willing and Motivated.

---

[9] Hsieh, Tony "Delivering Happiness: A Path to Profits, Passion and Purpose", *Business Plus Hachette Book Group, New York, NY* 2010

Tony Hsieh, the CEO of Zappos, followed his own blueprint in building one of the most successful online companies. And, when he knew it was time, he created another plan to sell it to a strategic buyer – Amazon bought Zappos for $1.2 billion. For Tony, his success in leading the company through this event had a great deal to do with his philosophy of happiness.

You need the 'what to do' and the 'how you will go about doing it' in your action blueprint. When you are about to embark on a major journey, it's very helpful to follow a map to which you refer repeatedly.

Let's learn more about the action blueprint; we'll lead you through the work of ensuring your company is profitable and saleable. As mentioned previously, there are four steps:

- Handle Reality
- Hone Goals and Decision
- Hunt Right Acquirer
- Helm Change

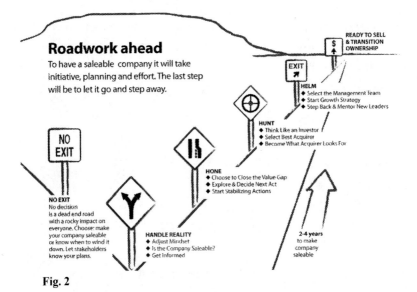

Roadwork ahead

To have a saleable company it will take initiative, planning and effort. The last step will be to let it go and step away.

READY TO SELL & TRANSITION OWNERSHIP

$

EXIT

HELM
- Select the Management Team
- Start Growth Strategy
- Step Back & Mentor New Leaders

HUNT
- Think Like an Investor
- Select Best Acquirer
- Become What Acquirer Looks For

HONE
- Choose to Close the Value Gap
- Explore & Decide Next Act
- Start Stabilizing Actions

NO EXIT

NO EXIT
No decision is a dead end road with a rocky impact on everyone. Choose: make your company saleable or know when to wind it down. Let stakeholders know your plans.

HANDLE REALITY
- Adjust Mindset
- Is the Company Saleable?
- Get Informed

2-4 years
to make company saleable

Fig. 2

Handle **Reality** – Learn how to determine if your company is saleable by exploring your mindset, current valuation, operational challenges and stakeholder concerns, so that you know where and how to make changes. Refer to your PlayBook: Answer items 1-3 and 5 in the Exploration Exercises in Chapter 1.

Hone **Goals and Decisions** – You will need personal goals, shareholder goals and company goals, as well as your personal philosophy to guide you. Setting goals requires making some difficult decisions and setting dates and timelines. You are taking on an entire new focus in preparing your company for sale. Letting go of your roles and trusting your employees to lead and manage may be one of the hardest steps in the process. It must be done at least a year before you are ready to engage a broker. Answer item 4 in the Exploration Exercise in Chapter 1.

Hunt **Right Acquirer** – By learning how to aim your company at the best target buyer, you will increase your chances substantially for being acquired, or being able to undertake a management buyout, or transfer of ownership to a qualified family member. Investors search for the key performance indicators that tell them your company fits their target criteria. Answer items 9, 10 and 11 in the Exploration Exercise in Chapter 1. Some of the prospects on your ideal acquirers' list may need a longer planning horizon, such as management buyouts.

Helm **Change** – This is the part of the blueprint that most owners don't recognize until it's too late to make material changes. If you understand the process involved in improving profitability and finding growth opportunities in today's economy, you will increase the company's value and, therefore, the amount a buyer may offer. Answer items 6, 7 and 8 in the Exploration Exercise in Chapter 1.

Even though, after working through the first Exploration Exercise, you ascertain that you have completed the work necessary for one of the steps, it's important to comprehend how all parts of this framework support the overall plan. Read about and then prepare a plan for all parts of the blueprint before making your final action decisions. By having a well thought out strategy for each step of your blueprint, you increase the probability of a buyer exhibiting more than just a passing interest in acquiring your company.

The Road to Succession Starts with You

Succession is such a hot topic today that there are many people selling proposals for various parts of this complex puzzle. There are wealth managers offering solutions for tax relief using holding companies and family trusts, seminars put on by investment bankers, mergers and acquisitions advisors, and business brokers explaining how they will help place your company 'on the market' for a fee. Bankers and accountants, as well as lawyers, provide great advice in support of lending you money.

Whom do you talk to first? What needs to be done first? Before you start delving into the complex world of mergers and acquisitions, you must start by preparing yourself. What you are about to discover will help you deal with your current reality.

To prepare you to start this personal exploration, you must start with your own level of motivation and develop your philosophy that will keep you going through the difficult parts. Human behavior tells us that nothing happens until you want to make it happen. Sounds simple enough, but many people are motivated by their routines rather than their aspirations – they often react to what comes at them, rather than by intention, to make big changes. The comfort zone of familiarity keeps more people on the couch than any other human motivation.

We notice that while many business owners say they want that exit plan, they are unaware of the changes they will have to make regarding how they think, interact, plan and take action in order to realize their objective. Human beings tend to take the road more traveled, the easy way out and the short cut. We are a nation of step skippers, unaware that the step just skipped is a vital lynchpin for gaining any foothold on the desired result.

What Type of Owner are you?

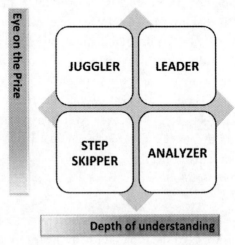

Fig. 3

Are you a 'get it done' type like many entrepreneurs? The problem is you start acting before you understand the underlying causes.

Step Skippers often solve the wrong problem with the wrong tool. Or, are you the type that wants to study the data and get all the analysis in before making a decision? 'Analysis paralysis' stops momentum and causes missed opportunities and lack of alignment. We also see many business owners struggle under the weight of too many things going on all at the same time.

Jugglers exhibit great zeal, but priorities are unclear and any crisis becomes the priority, so everything feels weighty, demanding and energy draining.

Leaders ask many questions and set up a master plan, sequencing the to-do list like a great project manager. You may want to ask trusted friends, colleagues or your spouse into which category you fall.

Each of these mindsets is a problem when facing the decision about whether to commit to building a saleability plan. If you do not know that part of the problem is how you think and then act on that thinking, then you won't spend your time learning to deal with what you don't know. And, therein lies your biggest barrier to making your exit dreams come true: your lack of awareness. The need to become aware of what you contribute to the effectiveness of your operation should be your top concern. If you don't know how you are ineffective, it will prevent you from getting curious to become attuned to learn first, plan second, and then act doing the right things correctly. *Effectiveness starts with how you frame a situation. What you think about, you get. But are you getting the right result?*

We have a saying regarding clients: if they are <u>aware</u>, <u>willing</u> and <u>motivated</u>, we take them on and help them to realize to their exit goals. <u>Aware</u> means to recognize that a problem exists. Are you aware you need an exit plan and don't know how to start? If you are aware you have a problem, then are you <u>willing</u> to spend the time to learn more about the nature of the problem and the options to deal with it? You are at the willing stage if you are reading this book, spending time searching the Internet and talking to trusted sources. Once you become willing, you start to understand the nature and dynamics of the problem, and you become keenly aware that you don't have the internal resources, knowledge, time or expertise to achieve your desired result. It's at this point that most people become <u>motivated</u> to look for the external catalyst that will drive the change needed to resolve the problem.

You can also apply this simple qualifying framework to your marketing strategies. Think about your own buying habits. If you do not need a car, you don't notice car ads. But, when your car starts to act up, or you decide you need to change your ride, you become willing to not only notice car ads, but you also take time out from other activities to do research on types of cars. When you are satisfied that you know what you want, you again set aside the time to select a method to purchase what you want and you work with someone to buy it. In fact, you make it a priority and the time to do it suddenly materializes.

Problem solved, change made!

When you need to make personal changes, such as get in shape or lose weight, your mirror may help make you aware you have a problem; however, it will not do anything to make you willing to take the time to research a plan for yourself. It's often an external event, such as the doctor telling you it's time to take action, that forces you to become willing and motivated to find, and begin a fitness and diet program. But what will keep you motivated if you aren't staring the doctor in the eyes? To stay motivated, you have to want the desired result more than the status quo. You need a personal philosophy of commitment that keeps you aligned with fulfilling your goals.

When it comes to the saleability question, specifically, do you want to take the time to make the changes to become saleable? If so, you first have to recognize and become aware you have a problem. The Handle Reality section is your first step to understanding the nature of the problem; nonetheless, only you can decide whether you want to do more than stare at the facts in the mirror.

The difficult truth about most companies is that they are not saleable because the owner, the CEO, the shareholder(s) or partner(s) are part of the problem and unaware of the facts. And, to become willing to do something about the problem, you first have to accept the truth of the situation before you ever become motivated to take action to become saleable. The owner will have to make the most significant changes. *It is your thinking and action habits that contribute the most to your current situation. Change how and what you think about, and change your reality.*

For example, learning how to recognize that what you built was designed to serve *you* rather than the company can be a significant leap. Your thinking habits may need to broaden, and your perception and awareness levels must deepen. Your ability to come to terms with the fact that what you built may have to change to be saleable is part of becoming aware, willing and motivated. You will be leading these changes; how you lead them will bring about your success or your struggle.

Recognize that building your awareness about the nature of the problems you might need to resolve, involves learning about aspects of your business that you didn't pay attention to previously. It's important to have some insights into how and why challenges exist in an organization. If you have challenges, then you know it is a sign that some changes need to be made to tune up and optimize the business in order to have it be attractive to buyers and financiers. A challenge is any dynamic that does not give you the result you want or need. Some are apparent and others cloak themselves in the everyday workings of the company.

You have been running your operation in a way that suits your style and needs, and the work of making a company saleable involves ensuring that it is operationally tuned for minimizing risk and maximizing returns for prospective buyers and customers. As you learn about the work of preparation, you will see your business with a different perspective.

Wear the Right Hat

The first step to gaining more awareness is to recognize what hat you are wearing. When you are the president of your company, you know what hat to wear. You run the company, and you are responsible to the shareholders for the return on investment, which is a direct result of the value you deliver to customers. Your job is to ensure the company remains a going concern and a great place in which to work, after you have gone. If you are also a shareholder, you wear a second hat, which requires you to shift your responsibility. As a shareholder, you are responsible for ensuring the president or managing partners deliver on planned goals and objectives, designed to achieve the desired return on investment.

If you wear both hats and you don't distinguish your role and responsibility when thinking and talking about the issues, confusion can abound for you and your employees. In some situations, there will be a definite conflict of interest between what is good for you as a shareholder and what the business actually needs.

As you move into the preparation for the exit, you now add a third hat and additional responsibilities to the first two. In addition to your functional hat and shareholder hat, you now have a personal hat seeking a happy financial future post sale.

If you also have a functional role beyond president, you add a fourth hat to your responsibilities that increases the complexity and potential for difficult decisions due to conflicting agendas. *Wherever you have a conflict, always put your president's hat on to gain clarity of understanding in order to make the right decision. When you take care of the company's short and long term interests in priority over any other agendas, everyone wins.*

Your shareholder hat responsibilities expand if you have multiple partners. You are now also leading the effort to get a deal that meets their objectives and expectations.

The responsibilities of each hat are often at cross purposes during the years leading up to an exit. Wearing the wrong hat as you think through a planning exercise can create conflict with another hat. For instance, wearing your personal hat and deciding you want $20 million for your exit fund, sets up an expectation that the company should be sold, so you get that amount when the deal is done. Unfortunately, what you have done is now become attached to that number. Maybe the company can't be sold for that amount without performing a lot of work that you must lead, or the effort to claim that wealth could compromise the integrity of the company. In that instance, it would be irresponsible for the president to pursue that strategic agenda. Perhaps your partners don't have the same aspirations as you and they want less . . . or, more.

Harmonizing all the needs of the different hats becomes possible when you pull out the interests, needs and requirements of each hat role separately. The best hat to wear is the one that takes care of the company so its future is secure. When you have certainty, you minimize risk. A profitable company attractive to buyers will take care of your personal shareholder needs far better than juggling hats back and forth. Keep your president's hat on from now on. As you work through the exercise of wearing the president's hat most of the time, you may uncover challenges that weren't apparent previously.

Wearing the right hat to explore what is needed and wanted may reveal operational or interpersonal dynamics that are not conducive to being saleable. You lived with these dynamics, but now they may become challenges that require solutions. Or, perhaps, you are aware these challenges existed, but you haven't found ways to minimize the effect of a challenge for the business.

Demystifying Challenges

Every business has challenges, and some of the challenges give the business its unique edge and are simply difficult to manage. In conversation, we often typify people challenges, such as a 'strong personality', and we view them as operational challenges. Moreover, we may answer such a challenge with the age-old cliché, "It's just the way things get done around here!"

Other types of challenges rob a business of its ability to be profitable by consuming productive time in an infuriating vortex of repetitive cycles. You can see the next collision coming before it's even happened because the pattern is predictable. These patterns are wrapped in the voices of complaints, judgements and irritations, and they are at the heart of the fires your managers attend to every day. This change-resistant vortex becomes what your employees struggle against, rather than spending their brain power capturing opportunities, realizing innovations or delivering rich customer experiences.

Most challenges are multi-dimensional and systemic, meaning they exist structurally. They are woven into the fabric of the culture and they persist because of interpersonal and personal dynamics, as well as the habitual ways of looking at and discussing the organizational problems. Many times, your greatest frustrations are a combination of challenges made complex by organizational process gaps (such as who is responsible for what and when), interpersonal barriers (such as personality traits that irritate you,) and personal thinking habits (such as thinking about what you *don't* want, not what you *do* want).

Organizational Structural Challenges

Structural challenges result when roles, responsibilities, accountability and performance expectations are unclear or not followed. Employees and even managers are unclear about who is supposed to do what, by when and for whom.

Secondly, the process for how paper and information flows through the organization is not well documented. To compensate for unclear or missing processes, employees develop their own 'systems' for getting things done. Individual systems are fine within a department, but when information has to flow across departments, any attempts at following a process breaks down, and the result is a chain reaction of constraints and unmet expectations.

Unfortunately, your staff will blame each other for the breakdown in the process. These chronic day-to-day struggles create interpersonal problems, and the process gaps often are found between accounting and operational departments, as well as between order fulfillment and manufacturing, or the front line customer service team and the back room operation team.

Organizational problems also grow when the management team is fragmented, rather than integrated in how they do their work. For example, if you have an important corporate initiative, don't send your people off to work on a piece of the plan on their own. While it seems like you would get it done faster that way, you are, in fact, skipping steps. Start together and share information together, so everyone has a full understanding of the problem. Then brainstorm the solutions to co-mingle all of the talent in the room. Your plan will be the better by taking the time to work collaboratively.

Lacking alignment and strong leadership communication while working to a set of prioritized plans, means managers work to the noisiest agenda. And, the result is organizational machinery that grinds instead of smoothly shifting through the daily gears.

Interpersonal Barrier Challenges

Interpersonal challenges occur when owners (shareholders, partners), managers and employees can't, won't or don't discuss process or people problems, opportunities or situations in a timely or effective manner. The truth of the problem is there, but the social structure or shared history won't allow the real contributors to the issue to be revealed, and the heart of the problem isn't dealt with once and for all.

Here's where most of us tend to believe that emotions have no place in the work environment. Yet every day, you see the effects of this silly idea burrowing holes in the best-laid plans. Of course, there are emotions among people; it's a myth that people can leave them at home. What we all do instead is pretend that we have no reactions to what others say or don't say, as well as how they say it. Factor in the water cooler conversations about what we're pretending doesn't happen, and now we have a grand recipe for poor productivity, poor performance and profitability leaks . . . all because we're supposed to pretend there are no emotions at work. And the Emperor has no clothes. Will you be the first to notice or the last?

As the owner, your emotions – said, unsaid, ignored or apparent for all to see – are the cues that your people use to make decisions. It's time to take responsibility for the emotions you put into the world, because if you don't, they come back to bite you. Become aware of your emotions – your anger (which is just a cover for not wanting to feel your fear and possibly being regarded as weak), your disappointment (also sounds like anger or frustration) and your hurt (which if you ignore, comes out sounding like cynicism, sarcasm and/or anger). That which you push away, manages what you do and how you think. So, if you really want to be a leader and manage to your desired result, listen to your emotions. Then you can learn from them and manage them.

Most interpersonal problems stem from ignoring the cause and effect of emotions, not mapping out how information should flow and lack of communication regarding setting priorities.

There are three common types of roadblocks in most of the companies with which we work and they create the following interpersonal problems:

Throw a Solution at the Problem: Rather than asking questions to get at the root of the problem, people tend to skip this step (too many landmines and they can appear to be too time consuming), and they throw a band-aid solution at a symptom of a problem that is not clearly defined. The most time consuming distraction will be to shoe horn a solution on top of a misunderstood problem, and you won't ever deal with the real issue and its impacts. I've listened to owners insist that if they just reorganize a department for the third time, that should fix the accounting issues. Instead of the knee-jerk response or repeating the same tactic that didn't work last time, meet with a cross-departmental team. Start with the end in mind – think of your desired result, such as accounting being able to issue invoices or close the books by the 10th of every month. Then, ask non-blaming, neutral questions of the team, such as "How does this work?" or "What happens when . . ." rather than, "Why did you do that?" Ask everyone involved to discover what does get accomplished, how it gets accomplished and collaborate to rework the process to get to the result you really want.

Point the Finger: Most challenges are systemic involving multiple people, departments and processes, rather than any one person or one department. The typical tendency to dismiss the person (new accounting manager?) does nothing to remedy the structural or interpersonal issue. In reality, most interpersonal problems are caused by structural challenges, such as accounting doesn't get the right information in time to do what is needed by the 10th of the month. Follow the instructions in Step 1, and then assess who needs to do what. Reassign roles, responsibilities and accountability for all the steps in the new process together with the people affected. Put them in the same room; don't reinvent the system on your own and instruct everyone to follow it.

Follow the Leader: Staff follows the example set by leaders. If leaders take action before exploring the nature of the problem, and they use that information to create a well-thought out plan with a clear, desired result, employees will do so, as well. If leaders tend to blame people (which emotion are you ignoring when you blame?), rather than searching for where the processes need redesign or clarification, the staff will react the same way. How often is it repeated that the accounting manager doesn't get it? If leaders look for what or who is wrong, rather than acknowledging excellent performance, the culture becomes steeped in negativity. And that blocks conversation about challenges. *Be the change you want to see in your attitude!* By leading in a way others can follow, you will gain Followership Intelligence (FQ)[10]. We will share more about using FQ to be a better leader a little later. Follow steps 1 and 2, and acknowledge everyone for working through the process with you.

Personal Challenges

Personal challenges arise from how a person thinks and which hat they wear while they're thinking. We are all affected by the nature and tone of our internal thinking, and we tend to think the same things repeatedly; and, it becomes an ingrained habit that takes greater self-awareness from which to break free.

For example, if we think about what we don't want, we tend to see evidence from conversations, ideas and actions around us that might lead up to that negative result, and we try to control people and circumstances to 'prevent' that event. If you wear a shareholder hat and perceive your fellow partners as being against selling or some other aspect involving a deal, you will listen for evidence of that in their tone, language and body language, and you will shape your response defensively.

Using a simpler example, think about what you say to yourself when you have lost something. "I can't find my keys." Or, "Don't forget to . . ." Then you experience not finding your keys and forgetting. Next time you lose something, try saying "I can find my keys!" or, "I will remember to . . ." This is called 'reframing to your desired end result'. It's not about reversing the negative statement to the positive statement; it's about stating the desired

---

[10] Carsten, Melissa K., Mary Uhl-Bien, Bradley J. West, Jaime L. Patera, Rob R. McGregor, "Exploring Social Constructions of Followership: A Qualitative Study" *The Leadership Quarterly 21 (2010) pp. 543-562* Elsevier Inc.

result you want. By telling yourself what you actually want, you unleash a very powerful tool that you can use to gain profoundly life-changing results every minute you choose to change (reframe) your thought pattern.

If we think about what we do want, we tend to see evidence from conversations, ideas and actions around us that might lead us to that desired result. Then, people respond to the vision you describe and they work with you to bring about the circumstances to actualize that result. What you think about, you get.

Interest and action follow intention.

Wearing your shareholder hat, if you think about having an agreement for a time, value and method that all shareholders buy into, and you trust that each shareholder will participate and reach agreement, then you will focus on that achievement and not say the things that create resistance or defensiveness.

As you practice reframing on the little frustrations in life, try it on the bigger, repetitive patterns that confound you in your business. Rather than responding with cynicism, for instance, the next time you go into a meeting and you hear yourself say, "Here we go again . . ." reframe it instead. Think, "What do I want to contribute in this meeting that will help us get results?" When you frame your internal thoughts with a question focused on what you do want, your brain will actually come up with ideas that flow with that idea, and your behavior will follow. Enter the meeting with cynicism and you give everyone permission to be cynical, too. Not a great atmosphere for a productive, positive meeting!

What would you rather spend your time thinking about? Game changing ideas that can catapult your team out of its habits, or looking for evidence that indicates that you are right? The same things are happening all over again. Every moment comes with a choice to reframe your thoughts into productive questions that change your actions and, even more important, how people relate to you – and follow your lead.

By committing to heightening your own awareness of how your feelings are affecting or infecting your thinking, you demonstrate to your employees how to do the same. You may not be aware that most employees read the facial and body language cues of the owner or boss to tell them how to respond. Think about what you wear on your face and body – if you're thinking about what you don't want and encourage yourself to doubt your people, they will act accordingly. People who don't feel trusted, don't bother making an effort.

When the boss smiles, notices effort, expresses compassion, or excitement, it gives everyone else permission to do the same with each other.

Using these tools will help you make the changes that will get your company in the running for the exit you really desire. Becoming aware of how the structural, interpersonal and personal dynamics create challenges in your company can be a relief for some owners. What you can see, you can do something about, especially if you practice using the suggested tools every day.

If you are like most business owners, once you understand how the problem occurs, that solutions exist to remedy the chronic challenges and you learn how the tools work, your willingness and ability to make the changes necessary to optimize operational performance increases exponentially. And, sometimes, just knowing that every company has similar challenges that can confuse best efforts can be the solace that drives the action.

Now that you understand the nature of how organizational challenges can obstruct profitability and optimization, you are better equipped to take a clear-eyed view of your company. The next exploration will help you and your partners, or family, get started on building the foundation for your blueprint toward your company becoming saleable.

Here is how it works:

The first Exploration Exercise helped you discover how ready your company is to be sold. This next exercise helps you discern how ready you are, personally, to move on from your role as business owner to leader of the transition of ownership. To get the most out of this exercise, set aside at least an hour, work in an area where you will have privacy and turn off all distractions. You may also want to take some of these questions to your spouse or friends to help you spark ideas. In fact, one of the best actions you can take is to sit down with friends and brainstorm about all of the things you could do in your future. Check the appendix for some great books to help your thinking.

Finally, make sure you are wearing the right hat when you answer these questions. The exercise is divided into three 'hat' sections. If you wear your functional hat while you are answering questions about your personal future, you may notice that your answers might be quite different. Let the 'right hat' stand so that you gain clarity.

Exploration Exercise #3
The Personal Exercise

PERSONAL HAT

1. When I sell my company, I want to take away $ _____.

2. My best guess is that my company is probably worth $ _____ today.

3. The difference between what the business might be worth (answer 2) and what I want to take away from selling the company (answer 1) is $ _____. This number is called the valuation 'Gap'.

4. I would like to sell in year _____; that is _____ months/years from now.

5. If there were a gap in value as discovered in answer 3, will I want to do what is necessary to prepare the company so it is worth more to a particular type of buyer? **Yes** _____ **No** _____

6. By preparing the company so it is saleable, I will be able to do the following things for myself and my family:

   _____

   _____

7. Post sale, I want to be able to:

   ☐ Keep working in my company for the new owners in order to build it to the next level in the role of

   _____

   ☐ Transition in a new leader and leave after _____ years

   ☐ Consult to the new owners

   ☐ Sit on the board

   ☐ Have no role in the company

   ☐ After I have sold my company, my next step in my life is to:

   _____

   _____

   ☐ The hardest part for me regarding selling my company will be:

   _____

   _____

8. If I can't sell my company, my back up plan is to (check all that apply):

   ☐ Continue as is

   ☐ Hire a manager to work under me

   ☐ Hire a president to run the company for me

   ☐ Sell to employees

   ☐ Find a partner and sell it to them over time

☐ Wind it down

☐ Keep going until it is saleable

☐ Learn about how to make it saleable

☐ Grow it until it is saleable

☐ Other (specify)

_____

9. My top preference(s) is to:

_____

10. If I can't sell my company for the amount that I really want, my back up plans for my exit fund financial needs are to (check all that apply):

☐ Sell it for the amount I am offered, even if it is lower than my desired number

☐ Reduce my financial requirements/lifestyle

☐ Consult back to the new owners of the company for additional income

☐ Get a job

☐ Invest it all and live off the interest, if possible

☐ Start another company

☐ Live in a country that has a lower cost of living

☐ Other (specify)

_____

11. My top preference(s) is to:

_____

_____

SHAREHOLDER HAT

12. If I (and, my shareholders) want to close the gap between what it is worth today and what I want to sell it for, it may take me 2 - 4 years to do this preparation and require

consulting with advisors to make changes. Am I willing to make that investment, time and effort?

Yes _____ **No** _____ If the answer is no, go to question 19.

13. Which of the following issues do you think may need to be addressed in your company in order for it to be saleable? Read through the following list and number them in order of priority.

_____ Profitability

_____ Management team

_____ Roles, accountability, authority, responsibility structure

_____ Goal setting and metrics

_____ Marketability of products/services

_____ Communications

_____ Thinking habits

_____ Emotional awareness

_____ Thinking about what I do want

_____ Internal systems and processes

_____ Organizational alignment

_____ Growth strategy

_____ Other (specify)

_____

_____

14. Do we have the right people in the right roles to make these changes, so that the work of making the company saleable will occur? Mark Yes, Not sure or No for each.

Company Leadership	(Yes	Not sure	No)
Department Leadership	(Yes	Not sure	No)
Operations	(Yes	Not sure	No)
Marketing/Sales	(Yes	Not sure	No)

Finance   (Yes   Not sure   No)

IT   (Yes   Not sure   No)

HR   (Yes   Not sure   No)

Manufacturing   (Yes   Not sure   No)

Other (specify)

FUNCTIONAL AND/OR PRESIDENT'S HAT

15. By preparing the company so it continues after I leave, I will be able to provide the following benefits for my:

Company

_____

_____

Employees

_____

_____

Customers

_____

_____

Suppliers

_____

_____

Family

_____

_____

Community

_____

_____

16. Knowing partners, the team and myself, the challenges that might make doing this preparation work difficult are:

Organizational (Structural Challenges)

_____

_____

Interpersonal Barriers

_____

_____

Personal, Emotional or Thinking Habits

_____

_____

Other

_____

_____

17. Looking at the challenges listed in your answers in question 16, place the challenges in the following categories to see if there are any dominant themes to determine which functional areas have challenges.

> Financial
>
> Product
>
> Service
>
> Supplier
>
> Customer
>
> Operations
>
> Systems
>
> Emotional and thinking habits
>
> People interaction
>
> Marketing
>
> Sales
>
> Existing agreements

18. Which area(s) of the operation has the most challenges? Check the top three that apply.

☐ Financial

☐ Product

☐ Service

☐ Supplier

☐ Customer

☐ Operations

☐ Systems

☐ Emotional and thinking habits

☐ People interaction

☐ Marketing

☐ Sales

☐ Existing agreements

19. What reactions do you have when you look at where your challenges are embedded? Write down your thoughts, feelings, frustrations, questions, concerns or doubts about each challenge area.

_____

_____

20. Check the box of the challenges that seem surmountable. You might want to explore how long these issues have been challenges in your company to answer this question.

☐ Financial

☐ Product

☐ Service

☐ Supplier

☐ Customer

☐ Operations

☐ Systems

☐ Emotional and thinking habits

☐ People interaction

☐ Emotional and thinking habits

☐ Marketing

☐ Sales

☐ Existing agreements

21. For which of these challenges do you think you may need another perspective or advice about learning why these issues exist and how to remedy them?

☐ Financial

☐ Product

☐ Service

☐ Supplier

☐ Customer

☐ Operations

☐ Systems

☐ People interaction

☐ Emotional and thinking habits

☐ Marketing

☐ Sales

☐ Existing agreements

There are no right or wrong answers. These questions are designed to help give you a baseline understanding of your current status, and to, perhaps, highlight areas that you had not thought about before wearing the right hat.

What was surprising to you? Are you more ready than you thought or less ready? Were you able to answer the questions easily or did they take time, or research, or were they unanswerable at this point? Make note of your realizations in your PlayBook now, so you can track them as you learn more, and note the changes in your willingness to do what is necessary to gain the exit you desire.

Wearing the right hat, let's discover what other aspects of your business may be more ready than you think they are.

Chapter 3 Summary

In this chapter you have come to terms, perhaps, with the current state of your inner and outer world. Remember, if you are aware of something, you can take appropriate action to change it. If you ignore it, the problem becomes your barrier to becoming both more profitable and saleable. By thoughtfully completing the Exploration Exercise and reviewing the challenges with which most companies struggle, you may have gained clarity and insights about what is important to you, as well as gained a sense of what a challenge is and how the dynamics play out within your organization. By wearing the right hat to answer these questions, you may have uncovered opportunities or gained insights that previously weren't possible to see.

Are you now more interested in learning about how to be prepared? Is your time shorter than the two-to-four years needed to prepare? There are many options for increasing your attractiveness for sale. As you find out what things you might be able to do in the short term that may bolster your attractiveness for sale, you may change some of your assumptions and decisions. You may also appreciate that your expectations for a sale at the price you desire may be limited, and that the type of buyer you can attract will also be limited.

At the end of the book, you will revisit this Exploration Exercise to help you refine your thoughts and responses based on what you learned, so you can decide what you really want after you've become informed. This final exploration will then become the starting point for your action blueprint. Then, we provide a quick start guide so you know which actions to take next.

Chapter 4
The Right Mindset & the Right Action

"New insights fail to get put into practice because they conflict with deeply held internal images of how the world works — images that limit us to familiar ways of thinking and acting. That is why the discipline of managing mental models — surfacing, testing, and improving our internal pictures of how the world works — promises to be a major breakthrough for learning organizations."

Peter Senge[11]

What you will learn in this chapter:

- How the conventional wisdom of some business practices actually contributes to poor performance, profit leaks and slow growth.
- The mindset adjustments that will set you up for success.

Now that you have discovered how close you are to having your company be ready for sale, and for you to lead the charge to that desired result, you need to be ready to start your learning journey on the right foot. Change can be difficult for some business owners, and if you want to be able to claim your wealth,

---

[11] Senge, Peter. "The Fifth Discipline: The Art and Practice of the Learning Organization". *Doubleday, New York, NY* 1990

you and your company will undergo some fairly extensive renovations over the next two-to-four years. You want to make sure that you are working with the right mindset to make useful and well thought out changes.

To become more reliably profitable and optimized with minimal challenges and, therefore, saleable, it is vital to wear the right hat:

- Adjust your mindset by evaluating the benefit or cost of following the shortcut to conventional wisdom

- Follow the action blueprint

The secret to becoming stable, profitable and saleable is all in how you perceive the inner workings of your company. You may have to reconsider some of the shortcuts you have taken, because that's what you thought was the right thing to do, or because other business people do it. Following conventional wisdom might not get you to your destination.

Are you guided by any of the following myths? It is time to get the facts straight about how your company can succeed even in a slow economy and meet your post-exit goals. As you have probably noticed, some companies succeed no matter what is happening in the economy and, in fact, many businesses start or accomplish their biggest leaps in growth when the pundits are busy convincing us nothing good is happening on the economic front.

Before any new learning challenge, it's best to set aside the idea that you already know what you are about to learn. If there is no room for new information, your journey won't start. It's time to become curious about what you think and what is required to be attractive to investors. Consider whether your mind is hijacked by any of these mindsets. Your belief systems, like challenges, can be hard to discern sometimes as they are already woven into your thought, habit and action patterns.

The Top 7 Mindset Adjustments for Success
Myth – I Can Sell My Company for What I Want

Investors buy future earning potential and look for past predictors, plus a sound written and emerging growth strategy to prove that potential. The methods that you use to value your company are probably not the same as those professional buyers and financiers use to determine an offering price. Learn to see the value points that buyers seek, and improve performance in those areas to get closer to the number you desire. Remember that becoming saleable and finding a willing buyer are two separate steps. Just because your company is saleable does not guarantee that you will find a buyer. It does, however, increase the probability.

Mindset Change

Learn to think like an investor (since you are the primary investor in your company), and view your company through that lens. Your perception of value may be very different from a buyer's perception. It won't help your case arguing with a prospective buyer to use your value criteria over theirs.

Myth – Similar Businesses are Offered the Same Multiples

Possibly. While it's true that each industry has a Multiple Range that buyers use to calculate an offer, Multiples have more to do with the state of your company in comparison to any other company. The Multiple that a buyer offers your company is based on a combination of the buyer's perceived risk and the opportunity the strategic fit promises, and/or the quality of the cash flow going forward.

Mindset Change

If you want to claim your wealth, take the time to learn how the Multiple approach may affect your choice of buyer, and then prepare you and your company accordingly. Don't make how long something takes become the top determinant in your decision to act.

Myth – All I Need is a Successor and a Wealth Plan

Your top priority is to make sure the business you are selling has all it needs to remain a going concern, bringing stable and growing returns to its next owner. Preparing your successors is second. Your personal wealth plan and tax strategies are conditional on what you can sell your company for and to whom.

Mindset Change

Focus on which type of organization or individual would most benefit from owning your business. Stand in their shoes and start highlighting the pros and the cons.

Myth – The Company Won't be Profitable and, therefore, Saleable Until the Economy Turns Around

Many companies are profitable, even in tough business sectors and industries despite the economy. Decide that your company will join their ranks and start looking at your operations with a different mindset. Cutting costs rarely solves the poor profitability complaint. Focus on what you *do* want, not what you *don't* want. It's not less money that you want to spend, it's more money that you want to bring in and retain. Costs generally remain fixed except for what goes into your products. What you really want to zero in on is making small increases in prices and volume. The result is much larger returns in gross margin and, therefore, profitability.

Mindset Change

Think about how to achieve growth in gross margin, rather than increasing sales and decreasing expenses. Even a 1% change upward in pricing without sacrificing volume contributes more to earnings than cost cutting. While you are making these changes, talk to current customers about how you can better serve their needs, and to prospects about what would make them switch to your products or services. Then start making those changes.

Myth – I Don't Have Time to Do All of This Optimization Work

You probably haven't run your business operation in a way that is optimized for investors. You've run it so it's optimized for your way of working, your convenience and personal return. It can be hard to imagine making myriad changes with which you are unfamiliar. Any long term goal, such as becoming more physically fit, learning a new sport or becoming saleable requires making sacrifices and taking risks in changing how and when you do things.

Mindset Change

Stay open to the possibilities while you are still in learning mode. Don't make the decision about whether you will commit to making your company saleable and to whom, until you have all the facts and have worked through the blueprint. Once you know what you want to achieve and why, it is suddenly much easier to make the time to implement your plan.

Myth – My Company is Successful, So I Can Sell It the Way It Is

Maybe. But wouldn't you rather know before you allow a business broker or acquisition advisor to shop it around to buyers, have them kick the tires, and leave you with nothing more than a lot of business cards and a hole in your personal productivity? Having interviewed numerous buyers who look at hundreds of companies every month about the lack of optimization done to be saleable and the thousands of dollars left on the table for lack of knowledge and effort, we know this mindset is highly detrimental.

Mindset Change

By working through this framework and building your blueprint, you will know with much greater certainty whether you might be well served making some optimization changes. Then your chances of finding a qualified buyer willing to entertain an offer grow substantially. With the flood of businesses on the market, buyers can afford to go after the pick of the litter.

Myth - If I Don't Do It, It Won't Get Done Right

Being indispensible or working alone without advisors or a management team, may have served you up to this point. Going forward, you are starting a new phase in life that requires learning, changing, trusting and making decisions based on new information. The plan for the future can't live inside your head. You may need to get the right people on the bus. You will need to lead this transition, so if you are still working in a functional role, you will want to empower your people to take more responsibility.

You will want to consult experts and integrate what they offer into your planning.

Mindset Change

Try on the idea that you are not the CEO or President any more. You are the primary investor in this company and mentor to your staff. To be a leader means to trust the people you have hired to achieve the goals you have set out, and to know when you need to bring in other perspectives and new information to augment your own. Invest the time to learn how to help your people be successful by showing them what to do *and* how to do it in order to meet your expectations.

With these mindset adjustments you will be able to do more than just operate your business – you will learn to see it with the eyes of a prospective buyer.

Armed with the right hat and being tuned in to what mindset adjustments you are contemplating, what does getting a business and its owners prepared for sale look like in action? You will find out as we examine closely whether Peter and his shareholders at PSWA are ready for sale.

Chapter 4 Summary

Preparing your company for sale means you will have to make many changes, and change can be uncomfortable. Learn to live outside your comfort zone, just like you did when you started this company. Letting go of old belief systems and ideas that get in the way of your success is vital to preparing your company for sale. Becoming comfortable with the uncomfortable, and even enjoying the ride, will make this work far more interesting and successful.

Which mindset adjustment is going to be the easiest for you to adopt? Some business owners may want to work with a coach who has the tools and experience to facilitate personal and operational transformation.

What will you need to do to make sure you make the adjustment? Review the following list and check those that apply in your PlayBook.

Now, what do you have to change in your personal thinking habits to adopt the new mindset? Set aside time to reframe your thinking toward the desired result you want for each mindset adjustment you checked.

- [ ] Myth – I Can Sell My Company for What I Want
- [ ] Myth – Similar Businesses are Offered the Same Multiples
- [ ] Myth – All I Need is a Successor and a Wealth Plan
- [ ] Myth - The Company Won't be Profitable and, therefore, Saleable Until the Economy Turns Around
- [ ] Myth – I Don't Have Time to Do All This Optimization Work
- [ ] Myth – My Company is Successful, So I Can Sell It the Way It Is
- [ ] Myth - If I Don't Do It, It Won't Get Done Right

Chapter 5
How Does the Blueprint Work?

"If you can't discover what's keeping you in, the will to get out soon becomes confused and ineffectual."

Daniel Quinn[12]

What you will learn in this chapter:

- How to apply what you have learned, to date, in a typical case study of a group of partners that is considering whether it is time to sell their company

- How thinking and communication habits can block a company's ability to come to terms with crucial business issues

- What a saleability action blueprint looks like

- The key elements that buyers and financiers seek, as well as those that signal that a company's investing worth

- The current state of the mergers and acquisitions market

One of the best ways to understand the concepts of saleability is to look at a case study. It's often easier to see the problems in another company than it is to look at your own. In this chapter, the case study will help you to recognize some of the dynamics with

---

[12] Quinn, Daniel. "Ishmael: An Adventure of the Mind and Spirit" *Bantam/Turner* 1992

which investors are concerned. Then there is another Exploration Exercise to help you understand, at a deeper level, your current thinking about your own firm.

A Case Study: The Profitability Struggle

Peter, Simon, Walter, and Andrea are all nearing sixty and together they forged a unique partnership, successfully growing a busy technical consulting firm (PSWA) into a multi-million dollar enterprise. Each partner is responsible for a different aspect of the business with Peter acting as CEO.

Nonetheless, for the last two years have had their problems.

In past years, there was money for dividends and bonuses, but, this year, one of them will have to tell the 200 employees the bad news – that even though they have worked hard all year and they are winning work when other firms are not, they are not making a profit. Why this is happening seems to be a perpetual mystery and, because of this, guessing the source of non-productive performance becomes a game to see who should shoulder the blame this week.

Everyone locks their eyes onto the CEO, Peter, who states that if they hadn't had so many un-billable hours on three or four projects in the last two years, as well as a big legal bill over a shareholder agreement, they could be paying themselves dividends, as well as bonuses to employees.

Simon suggests that it's all because they aren't managing projects properly – and that is why their $35 million company can't pay a 3% bonus. Then, Walter, who is head of projects, refutes Simon by saying that the problem is in Andrea's department. She invested in excessive hiring last year in Accounting, HR and IT.

Peter notes Andrea's irritation and slouches back in his chair, drained. He suddenly realizes that with the constant tension among the partners, their 'pass the blame' mentality, in addition to the same old problems year in and year out, they never seem to resolve any one problem. They need to keep winning new work and, because they can't guarantee new projects these days, they've dropped their rates and they have to accept any project just to ensure they can make payroll.

> "Annual income, twenty pounds; annual expenditure, nineteen pounds; result, happiness. Annual income, twenty pounds; annual expenditure, twenty-one pounds; result, misery." Charles Dickens

With this economy, it seems that the pressure of having to deal with uncertainty influences every decision.

The question of selling comes up in Peter's mind.

Peter wonders if the company might be worth $15 million or $20 million. It might be a big enough number that it would bring some consensus of action among his partners.

Hence, his lunch meeting with the advisor.

From what you have learned so far, do you think PSWA, Inc. is saleable in its current state? What would happen to the interpersonal dynamics at PSWA, if Peter suggests they can sell the company for $15 million to $20 million? Owners often attach themselves to a speculative price with little understanding of what it takes, realistically, to sell a company for that price. When this attachment grows, it's difficult to dislodge, so owners find it hard to deal with a reality that doesn't support this valuation. This attachment can turn into a blind spot that skews opportunities for selling – at any price.

Get Informed!

To an outsider, it may look as if PSWA simply needs a competent leader who is willing to take charge, in order to work out any operational issues. What these partners *actually* need is education and awareness building, so that they lead themselves through myriad systemic changes that are necessary to be profitable. They need to understand exactly how their company earns and loses money, and they need to carve out a stronger market niche to defend higher charge-out rates. A strong leader is essential to achieve these changes; their next step is to become willing to obtain that help – not toss around potential valuation numbers. Nonetheless, who will help them gain this awareness, so they stop playing the blame game and start learning how to deal with this problem?

These shareholders have a decision to make. They must want to learn how to become aware. They must stop blaming each other about their realized results, which keep alive the mystery regarding why their company is unprofitable. Their willingness to face facts and get the right kind of support, advice and guidance will save a lot of time and money. The longer they stay in the blame game, the more money all investors lose, and the harder it is for the company to recover.

Let's return to PSWA as a model, to give you an idea of its plan of action, as well as how you may take some ideas and tailor them to your company.

What does their company need from them, as shareholders?

Wearing their shareholder hats, they must explore and understand the viability of attempting to find a buyer, and complete a transaction within six to twelve months.

The reality is their chances of success are slim. It's difficult to find a buyer who purchases technical consulting firms that aren't profitable, don't have predictable and stable or growing revenue, or who don't have a unique market niche, in addition to an installed and capable management team that is committed to a feasible growth strategy.

So, in addition to Handling the Reality of their situation, wearing both of their shareholder and functional hats, each partner must gain clarity of their own personal goals. The results of these two explorations will help them become realistic regarding which type of acquirer they need to seek.

Putting their shareholders' needs in perspective, they must then factor in the reality of what the company must achieve to be worth the shareholder's financial goals *and* be attractive to a buyer. They can then put on their functional hats to determine if the work and changes needed are feasible. Then, it's time to realize what kind of leadership PSWA needs from them in order to Helm the Transition.

PSWA Saleability Blueprint

Handle Reality

- Analyze financial statements and follow instructions to determine the company's current value
- All partners agree on wanting to sell, when to sell, and how to prepare the company to attract a buyer
- Find an advisor to teach them how to see their business differently
- Uncover their challenges and decide to remedy them

Hone Goals

- Set personal, shareholder and functional goals
- Get needed advice for each goal type

- Set strategic vision and company goals
- Assign development of action plans to managers

Hunt Acquirer

- Determine the type of buyer they want to pursue and how to engage that buyer
- Resolve whether the right people are in management based on acquirer type
- Hire VP of Financial Management, to lead accounting and set key metrics
- Hire or train successors for all partners' roles, who are given the goal of attracting a strategic buyer
- Add strategic goals and plans that help the company be more attractive to the targeted buyer

Helm Transition

- Integrate strategic goals and plans into daily actions
- Assign responsibility to achieve goals to managers
- Increase charge-out rates for all new clients
- Ascertain where the company may gain slight changes in rates and cost recovery. Think 1-5% not 10%.

These actions represent a full blueprint for action for a company like PSWA on all four elements of the framework for saleability. Your blueprint may have additional actions based on your industry and company needs, as well as the type of buyer you will hunt.

Profitability is one of the key metrics that counts. Investors seek companies with consistent and growing profits over the last eight to twelve quarters, but PSWA is not profitable because of the way it is managed and their inability to recognize and deal with their challenges. In fact, the reasons they are not profitable are interrelated across all the actions in the blueprint. Each element that they put into action will increase productivity and performance, which leads to greatly improved profitability.

If PSWA learns how to make a profit and does the work to solidify their operation and internal interaction, their chances will improve dramatically.

PSWA's Next Step

PSWA isn't profitable, so it isn't the best time to sell. The partners may find buyers interested in 'distressed' companies (the term that financial buyers use for companies in financial trouble). However, investors are not likely to offer the price company owners are seeking. It *is* the best time for PSWA to invest in coaching, consulting and acquiring advisors; they must help the shareholders discover what is not working, and enact the blueprint to build value and profitability.

Peter and his team will want to invest in developing metrics to point out which operational components of the company are causing the cash flow problems and profitability issues. (You can have cash in the bank and still not be profitable, or, appear to be profitable on paper, but not have the cash to pay bonuses or pay down the credit line.)

Controllers keep companies in compliance with Generally Accepted Accounting Principles (GAAP) while a financial management specialist helps you make well thought out financial decisions while managing the accounting department. You may need both to work through all of the financial issues.

PSWA also needs to work closer with their banker to obtain support resources and manage a growing line of credit. PSWA, like many companies, has an operating line of credit to bridge cash-flow gaps to make payroll. While they have not reached their credit limit, with declining revenues (due to reducing their rates and loss of key clients), that situation may change this year. Peter and his partners need to understand the contributing factors placing stress on their cash flow, before they can strategize a solution.

They need to keep their bankers in the loop. Banks provide many options to help companies like yours and PSWA. But, the bank can't change how the company manages projects to keep clients happy and loyal, increase work quality or help partners resolve long-standing conflicts that block their ability to fix operational frustrations. However, they can provide you with the resources and introductions to people who can help. They will also suggest a number of strategies to improve cash management, such as shortening invoicing cycle times to increase cash flow.

Cutting back on key hires made the previous year will not resolve PSWA's cash flow or profitability problem – getting charge-out rates back to previous levels with current and new clients will, however. Better project quality standards and management's overseeing the staff's time working on projects will improve profitability and make PSWA the better company with which to do business, thereby allowing the rates to increase.

All of the partners are functional managers who are working alone in their silos. Their managers need clear guidance from the partners on the company's vision. Where do they want to stake their claim in the market? How big do they want to become? What do they want to be known for? These goals then need an integrated set of plans in addition to working collaboratively on cross-departmental problems, such as quality standards, billing cycles and gaining new clients. These are key organizational issues that require everyone rowing together.

As with the shareholders in PSWA, these are items that owners need to question – not in order to be able to sell, but to be profitable in the meantime.

However, before we work through building your own blueprint, you may first want to know more about the current environment for selling companies such as yours.

The Investor Marketplace

No matter the state of the economy, there will always be investors looking for great acquisitions. You may think that buyers will look for reduced priced deals; however, while it may be counterintuitive to think otherwise, investors are still buying companies at high prices even in a slow economy.

What you might not know is that investors look for companies with reduced risk profiles in which to invest, rather than what we might think of as 'good deals'. 'Reduced risk' means that they can see exactly how a prospective company will continue to earn, grow and prosper in the future, because that is what is occurring today. So, while our economy might not grow as it did several years ago, there isn't any reason why that should stop your company from being the most productive. Especially if you want to be one of those good deals an investor seeks, so you can sell your company.

While profitability is good for business, the bank and employees, your company needs more than that to help secure your own vibrant future. You can't wait for a buyer to make an offer, or wait until the day you are too tired or dispirited to make the right improvements to be attractive for sale. There is a big change in the balance between demand for acquisitions and the supply of low-risk investments. Aging boomer business owners are putting their companies on the market in record numbers, and investors have a plethora from which to select.

Here is a rundown on the cold, hard facts to prove to you why action is imperative.

Your company is one of 3,200,000 mid-market companies in North America who want to extract retirement wealth over the course of the next 10 years. (a combined $10.4 trillion of net worth, according to Robert Avery[13]) According to GW Equity (September, 2006), 75% of your cohorts hope to sell even sooner.

In a given year, and within the private mid-market deal space, there are approximately 13,000 businesses that change hands through Brokers, Mergers and Acquisition Advisors or Investment Bankers[14]. Uncounted are those sold to a trusted employee(s) at a steep discount, and those that just close or wind down.

The greatest contributor to wealth destruction is to 'gift' an operating business to a family member.[15] While 40% of family-owned business owners hope to pass the reins over to the next generation,[16] only 40% of family-owned businesses survive the second generation.[17] This is because family members often are not qualified to lead a company, and/or the knowledge transfer is poorly planned.

It's a buyers' market. There are multiple bids on some businesses and none on others. Just like the housing market in a strong economy, owners have a greater probability of selling an un-optimized company or a house that isn't updated. In today's economy, this probability decreases substantially and buyers are much more discerning, because business risks are much greater and they enjoy more selection from which to choose.

---

[13] Avery, Robert. "The Ten Trillion Dollar Question: A Philanthropic Game Plan" *Cornell University* 2006

[14] Capital IQ, March 2010

[15] Deans, Tom "Every Family's Business"

[16] Poza, Ernesto. "Heirs and Graces in Family Business" *Business Week August 11, 2003*
http://www.businessweek.com/smallbiz/content/aug2003/sb20030811_8446_sb013.htm

[17] Deans, Tom

By doing the preparation, you'll stand out from the crowd, you will sell faster and get much closer to the number you really seek. You'll also leave your community, employees, customers and suppliers with a valuable legacy of economic health and contribution long after you have made your exit.

The choice is yours.

Research done by BMO Financial Group[18] on US and Canadian business owners' attitudes and preparation for succession in their businesses, as well as that done by the Canadian Federation of Independent Business,[19] shows that owners are unaware of these facts and they don't realize they have choices for dealing with this seismic market shift. If your retirement income is dependent on your selling the biggest asset you ever owned, consider how you want your company's value to be perceived. What is the biggest contributor to company value erosion? It's suddenly deciding that you want to sell your company in the next six months to a year without having prepared adequately. We've met many owners who unwittingly stepped into this big pothole because they did not plan effectively, and could only see the finish line, not the next step on the road or the dynamics of the race.

> The biggest contributor to company value erosion is deciding you want to sell your company in six months to a year, without adequate preparation.

---

[18] BMO Financial Group. "BMO North America Business Study: Canadian Business Owners More Upbeat On Economy Than U.S. Counterparts" October 2010.

[19] Bruce, Doug and Derek Picard "Succession can Breed Success" *Canadian Federation of Independent Business* 2005 http://www.cfib-fcei.ca/english/research/canada/224-business_issues/251-succession_can_breed_success.html

While the economy remains an uncontrollable variable, improving operations and market positioning are entirely under your control; and, once you are aware of the necessity of completing your preparation work and finding the motivation to learn how to do it, you'll be on your way to successful and profitable succession.

Not all businesses need optimization to be saleable; however, if you are gaining awareness that yours could use tuning up in order to meet your valuation expectations, what's in store for you and your employees?

Chapter 5 Summary

In this chapter, we opened the black box on the inner gears of a typical company. It's rare for most business owners to get a look under the hood of another business to see why the engine pings, why mileage isn't efficient and why the car veers left. Given these dynamics, it becomes apparent that this company bases its poor results on systemic problems – it's not any one person's fault. The blueprint for dealing with these issues may seem daunting, but each element can bring motivational rewards and inspire the next step.

It's a buyers' market.

To stand out, an owner will want to ensure they become the cream of the crop in their industry if they want a financial or strategic buyer to acquire them.

Chapter 6
The Work of Preparation

Great things are done by a series of small things brought together.

Vincent van Gogh[20]

What you will learn in this chapter:

- The difference between actual value and perceived value, and how to reconcile the two numbers
- How to plan for your next act in life
- How to work toward getting ready for sale in two ways
- The work you need to do, personally, which is more like preparing for a journey
- The work you need to do in your operation, which is similar to remodelling a house.

Combine these and you are building a bridge between today and the day you deposit the check that will fund your great retirement or exciting next act.

---

[20] Vincent William van Gogh (30 March 1853 – 29 July 1890) was a Dutch post-Impressionist painter

The amount of work that you need to do in order to motivate you and your operation depends on your state of mind as it relates to:

- The emotional and mental shape of you and your partners
- How much effort you want to put into closing the gap between what your company is worth today and the exit value you really want.

If you have partners, their responses to these questions, as well as the Exploration Exercises you have completed so far, must be reconciled with yours. It adds a layer of complication if you and your partners have differing goals and energy levels, or you are unwilling or unable to address some of the challenges you uncover.

Educating yourself affords the best protection in these uncertain times. If life throws you a curve ball, being prepared is your best insurance policy for success.

What's Your Secret Number?

Every owner has a 'secret number'. This is the number they want in return for selling the business once they've examined revenues or sales, done the math, compared valuations with other deals they have heard about, and tested out the sound of that particular number with friends, partners or family. Social proof may validate the number in your mind, but it can be a pothole when it comes to handling reality.

The internal dialog often goes like this, "If I got $X million for the business, sure I'd sell." An attachment to that specific number begins to grow.

There is a different, more realistic number in another compartment of the brain, and it's the number an owner thinks the business is really worth – the bad news is it's usually lower than the secret number. This is the counter balance number that keeps feet on the ground and the ego in check.

But, it's the secret number that can get some owners in trouble. Using Peter at PSWA as our example (who initially had done a quick calculation and come up with a number he thinks might be large enough to stop the bickering among his partners), we can see the problem brewing. He announces a number that will instantly evoke visions, hopes and dreams. Now, the partners attach themselves emotionally to Peter's number, which may bear little relation to the company's true worth. Unfortunately, the secret number is an unrealistic expectation. Today, Peter's company's worth is nowhere near his secret number. He has set up a big valuation gap and he has inadvertently set them up for failure before they have even begun. The difference between their secret number and the company's worth today is what we call the 'valuation gap'. Closing that gap requires they recognize that there *is* a gap, and then they must uncover what they need to do to remedy their problems with their action blueprint.

In fact, the number one reason buyers give when asked why they don't acquire more companies is the owner's unrealistic expectations about company worth, as well as unwillingness to learn about or recognize why this discrepancy in value exists. The secret number attachment makes deals fall apart at the negotiation stage.

If you are serious about selling, keep a reality check on what your company is really worth – today! The number you set drives your decisions and either allows you to get to your destination or leads you to dead ends, thereby eliminating the possibility of closing a deal. Knowing how your feelings motivate and de-motivate you is the primary part of preparation, followed by the actual financial reality check. All decisions and preparations need to correlate directly with understanding the amount of money your company is actually worth, as well as what an investor will realistically pay, as opposed to what you ideally want for it. The difference between these numbers is what we call the 'gap'.

You <u>can</u> choose to do something about closing the gap two-to-four years prior to when you want to sell, so you get closer to your secret number. Remaining attached to your secret number and not doing anything operationally has ruined more deals at the last minute than we can count.

Are You Ready for a Valuation Reality Check?

A reality check has two components:

- to reconcile your perception of what your company is worth, and
- to anticipate investors' perception of your company's value.

Sometimes, these two perceptions turn out to be quite far apart.

Chances are you have put your best years into building your business, working through incredible challenges and riding out the highs and lows that result in many loyal and valuable clients with years of buying history. They back up your perspective about the value of your company. Taking this time to acknowledge all of your efforts to build your business into what it is today is a vital part of becoming ready for your exit.

All of the creative energy, mentoring, leading, innovating and coaxing you have invested requires appreciation; however, no one followed you around for the last 20 or 30 years to witness everything you did to make this a great company. Your past effort does not equal enterprise value (what a buyer is willing to offer), no matter how much you argue for it.

For your own wellbeing, *never confuse the perceived value offered by a potential buyer with the effort you have invested in it.* You must separate these perceptions because one is what you have built and it has huge value to you (emotional), and the other concerns the future value that will be harnessed by someone else (financial). The investor buys the opportunity to receive future profits based on what you have built, and the new owner shapes those sales and profits.

The amount of money a buyer is willing to pay is dependent on:

- How investors value the future profit potential versus the perceived risk
- How 'tuned' your business is to the right market
- How quickly investors are able to realize the desired future value

As you learn to appreciate the differences in applying the concept of 'value', you will be able to see your business from the investor's perspective. Remind yourself of the difference between past and future value to keep yourself sane, and allow yourself to let go of your past role as CEO, owner and President in order to move painlessly through this transition in your new role as an investor.

Your Next Act

One of the most important steps in letting go of your role as business owner, leader and president is to start to see a rosy future for yourself; however, it means more than daydreaming about golf or traveling. You have been a valuable and contributing member of society for quite some time, and to stop simply because you have sold your company is unnecessary and harmful to your health and wellbeing.

Today's boomer isn't interested in retirement. You want a more vital and meaningful life, free from the confines of daily business. Company owners have gone on to vibrant and fascinating lives post sale. Here's a sample of what is in store for you when you have the money and the time to invest in exploring how to contribute:

- Teaching at a local or foreign university
- Becoming a master gardener
- Building a boat and sailing to other parts of the world
- Becoming a spokesperson for a cause
- Serving as a mentor to other business owners
- Joining an angel investor network
- Running for office
- Sitting on other company boards
- Learning to paint
- Starting a garage band
- Designing products
- Serving as a volunteer executive overseas
- Building a house
- Becoming expert in a sport
- Writing a book on your expertise
- Becoming a speaker on your topic
- Working for your industry association
- Going on vocational vacations
- Finding and developing your creative skills
- Raising your grandchildren to support your busy kids

Reinventing yourself is a big part of this journey to the exit. If you have something you are looking forward to doing or being, then you are more likely to stay the course. There are many ways to reinvent yourself, but some exploration might be your best investment, so that you really understand what you want and need. Remember, you have been immersed in the day-to-day drama of your work world for a long time. Parts of you may have been switched off in an effort not to interfere with your need to be functional.

Look at the resources in the Appendix and in your PlayBook to find some ways to start your reinvention program.

Chapter 6 Summary

A valuation gap can exist when an owner believes their company is worth more than a buyer may agree to pay. The gap exists because owners want their company's value to be based on their years of hard work, emotional investment and opportunity costs or sacrifices they have made.

Investors take a very different view of value. Owners must focus on the investors' view of value and, if there is a discrepancy between this number and the number with which the owners hope to walk away, they must reconcile themselves to the fact there is work to accomplish in order to optimize the business.

Setting personal goals for yourself and taking the time to build a bright future is part of the journey of being ready to sell your company. Take the time to envision fully how you want to live in your next act so you serve your core needs.

Chapter 7
How Much is My Company Really Worth?

"Price is what you pay, value is what you get."

Warren Buffet[21]

What you will learn in this chapter:

- How investors perform a valuation
- Understanding the term 'Multiple'
- How to perform a rough valuation of your company
- Understanding perceived risk

Company valuation is subjective to the owner and objective to the buyer. Value is in the eye of the buyer, and learning to think like an investor builds your objectivity, so you can appreciate its value in ways other than your own subjective view. Working through this exercise is an essential survival skill and an excellent strategy to use in the letting-go process.

Looking down the road, consider that your company may be saleable but, perhaps, not for the amount you want in its current state. *Why do we say that when we know nothing about your company?* Because experience dictates how investors think and

---

[21] Warren Edward Buffet (30 August 1930) is an American investor and CEO of Berkshire Hathaway

how they decide on what is valuable to them. We talk to many brokers, investment bankers, advisors and buyers who are frustrated with the lack of optimization done by owners!

Valuation Methods

There are two types of value:

- Fair Market Value, and
- Investment Value.

Fair Market Value refers to an arm's length review of the assets of a company, thereby arriving at a true reflection of a company's worth. *Investment Value* is what a motivated buyer will pay to acquire the company.

There are many types of valuation methods to determine investment market value. Buyers have their own levels of value and methods to assess a firm's financial health and attractiveness, and each value point is measured against a set criterion. Aspects that don't match their value level are discounted or elevated to a premium from the base price that a buyer might offer.

There are several approaches that professional valuation specialists use to determine the value of a firm. However, there are also simpler tools to give owners an easier metric to gain a sense of their company's value. These simpler methods are what we will describe here.

We will use a Multiple approach method to give you a reality-check about what your business might be worth today. But it's not a definitive valuation of your company. If you want to invest the money to know exactly what your company is worth today, use a Certified Valuation Specialist. For our purposes in demonstrating the size of your valuation gap, such an investment is not required. Recognize that when you are ready to put your business on the market, your M&A advisor will use several approaches to determine value, so don't get attached to exact numbers at this stage of your journey.

The Multiple Approach

A Multiple is the term used by valuation experts to describe an observed trend in the selling price of businesses, and each industry has its own set of Multiples based on Multiples previously paid to similar businesses. Technology companies tend to receive offers with the highest Multiples; service-based businesses and un-optimized companies receive the lowest. The Multiple number is the additional value applied to a financial indicator such as revenue, profit, or discretionary earnings. Using a Multiple to value a business is a shortcut based on the simplification of more in-depth valuation methodologies. Remember that they do not substitute for a comprehensive valuation analysis. It only provides a guideline for the price of the average business in a particular industry, without consideration of any unique attributes.

The Multiple-based approach does, however, provide a ballpark value of your company, so you can determine how close or far you are from the amount for which you want to sell. The Multiple a buyer offers is based on specific industry market conditions, comparable acquisitions, the desired rate of return, and, most important, the operational health and future of a company. The buyer then multiplies this number by the last 12 months of profit, or gross margin, or sales of your business depending on their chosen approach. Our example uses profit defined for Multiple-Based Approach to valuation as 'earnings before interest, taxes, depreciation and amortization', commonly known as 'EBITDA'.

As you start this reality-check exercise, don't be tempted to do a 'normalization' adjustment to add back to your EBITDA (those one-time costs you think won't reoccur in subsequent years) on your own or even with your accountant. It is more useful to work with your real EBITDA without doing an adjustment. Like the secret number problem we discussed in the last chapter, adding back can become a calculation game rather than a serious reality-check exercise. When it comes time to put your company on the market, your valuation expert, business broker, M&A advisor or investment banker will help determine the add-backs to include in an effort to normalize earnings.

Many buyers will want to see how you calculate your EBITDA and know what you normalized as profit to get a better financial picture. Realize that if you get to the due diligence stage, you will have to prove all of your justifications. The more 'accounting re-engineering' you do, the more difficult it becomes to see the business clearly, so it's best to leave the normalization strategy to the experts.

Comparing EBITDAs in Your Industry

You can find the expected EBITDA for a company in your specific industry by reviewing the averages on the website listed in the Appendix to see where your company ranks, as well as in the recent data from Capital IQ in Figure 4.

Multiples in 2004 - 2006, were very high in many industries – high tech companies were getting 15 + x EBITDA, and industrial companies with average earnings might have received offers of 8 + x. In today's slower paced economy, a similar industrial company with predictable cash flows, solid market share and a growth strategy might be lucky to get an offer of 7 + x.

These are the norms in a struggling economy.

Capital IQ March 2010 Analysis of Mergers and Acquisitions FOR COMPANIES LESS THAN $500 M IN VALUE					
	STRATEGIC BUYERS		FINANCIAL BUYERS		AVERAGE
	last twelve months		last twelve months		MULTIPLE
Sector	2009	2010	2009	2010	2009	2010
Consumer discretionary	1,631	1,542	362	302	9.8X	8.1X
Consumer Staples	313	282	56	47	7.9X	10.1X
Energy	636	928	36	27	6.8X	5.6X
Healthcare	902	892	83	66	15.1X	10.1X
Industrials	1,661	1,481	240	162	8.8X	8.6X
Information Technology	1,667	1,602	145	113	11.2X	10.6X
Materials	870	1,065	99	58	7.9X	9.3X
Telecommunications Services	104	101	10	4	6.4X	7.0X
Utilities	148	186	10	6	8.3X	8.1X

Fig. 4

The graph in Figure 4 shows the number of deals completed in each sector by strategic buyers and financial or private equity buyers, as well as the average Multiple paid for companies across both buyer types. Buyers use this data to compare the value of deals they are looking at in the same way realtors might compare similar houses in the same market. A company with profit fluctuations, cash flow or market uncertainties, or no particular brand leadership or differentiation will have 'points' taken off the 'Multiple x EBITDA' offered. *Points represent the value that your company has built.* An investor who sees risks in a company is not prepared to pay as much for the value; risk is the antithesis, or opposite, of value. A 'point' reflects the buyer's ability to understand and 'see into' the business. If they can see clearly how a company meets customer needs, how it produces predictable cash flow and how probable growth can be achieved, 'points' in the Multiple applied can be validated and sometimes increased.

For instance, Figure 4 represents the average Multiples[22] paid on deals worth less than $500 million in the U.S. over the last four years. Companies in similar industries in Canada, tend to earn smaller Multiples. Remember that buyers are interested in optimized companies. The less optimization, the greater the risk for the buyer, the smaller the Multiple offered.

The Multiple Scorecard

Once the buyer has a Multiple in mind, typically they review your business against a set of criteria to guide their acquisition decisions. They ascribe points to a range of issues and develop a scorecard. The highest valuation is given to companies that 'earn' the greatest number of points on their scorecard. Typically, points are deducted for areas of risk:

- they can't accurately forecast

- access to critical skill is limited or unavailable and information or knowledge essential to the continued well-being of the company and its future growth prospects isn't clear or provided

For every demerit, the Multiple number may be reduced by a fraction of a point, i.e. from a Multiple of 6.75x, to a Multiple of 6.25x.

In the following example, the buyer evaluates a firm based on many variables. The buyer obviously likes the product offering as they have rated it a 5 out of 5, but there are concerns about the company's growth potential. More troubling is their evaluation of the management team, rated a 3 out of 5. Perhaps the current managers do not have enough experience to lead growth. Or, even more common these days, these remaining managers have tremendous experience, but they are getting close to retirement,

---

[22] Data from Capital IQ Market Observations January 2011

thereby making their current value high, but limited into the future.

If the owners state that employees and managers remain employed by the new buyer, but the buyer raises concerns about their ability to grow the company, owners must decide how important it is to keep the company intact post-acquisition or to let people go in order to sell. Knowing that these parameters are on an investor's mind, a well-prepared owner can resolve these management issues now before the firm is put on the market. This advanced planning can improve the score, resulting in a higher multiple and, therefore, it potentially justifies (all other dynamics being equal) the expected enterprise value. This is an effective step toward closing the gap between what your company is really worth and your secret number.

ACQUISITION EVALUATION SCORECARD Score 1-5 (5 being excellent)	Example Company Scoring	Your Company's Scoring
INDUSTRY ISSUES	19/25	
Economic	2	
Geographic	5	
Uncontrollable Variables	4	
Ethical	5	
Buying Trends	3	
INDUSTRY ISSUES TOTAL		
BUSINESS ISSUES	40/50	/50
Product/Service offering	5	
Scalability	4	
Product life cycle	3	
Uniqueness of offering	5	

Market niche	4	
Growth potential	3	
Legal	5	
Environmental	3	
Diversified Revenue	4	
Distribution	4	
BUSINESS ISSUES TOTAL	19/30	/30
MANAGEMENT		
Personality & Culture	3	
Expertise & Skill Sets	3	
Time frame of commitments	3	
Experience & Depth	4	
History of Success	2	
Ability to communicate effectively	4	
MANAGEMENT TOTAL	21/30	/30
FINANCIAL		
Stability of Cash Flow	4	
Predictability of Revenue	4	
Use of leverage	2	
Quality of Revenues	4	
Gross margin growth	3	
Variability of costs	4	
FINANCIAL TOTAL	25/30	/30
DEAL RISKS		
Lack of exit options	4	
Strength of 5 year plan	5	

Ability to communicate effectively	4	
Added value to current activities	5	
Risk of Loss of value post acquisition	3	
IRR	4	
DEAL RISKS TOTAL		
TOTAL SCORE	124/165	/165
GRADE AS A PERCENTAGE	76%	

Fig. 5

In Figure 5, the acquisition target receives a 76% score from the buyer after a first review and before a letter of intent or due diligence. With a perfect score of 100%, the company might have earned a higher multiple depending on their industry. For example, if this were a manufacturing company in an industry that had averaged 8X Multiples, a buyer might reduce their offer from 8X to 6X (76% of 8). With an EBITDA of $5 million in the past 12 months, the owner of this manufacturing firm might receive a letter of intent and an offer for $30 million ($5 million EBITDA x 6X). If they had done their preparation work to optimize the company in the years leading up to this offer, the Multiple and/or the EBITDA would have increased. Then the owner might have received a higher offer. Consider, though, that the manufacturing firm also had to meet the buyer's profile criteria to merit a higher Multiple. Your conclusion? Value is subjective, which the owner can't change. Value is also based on facts that the owner can do a lot to change before putting the company on the market.

Concern About the Internal Rate of Return

Investors want to acquire at a price where they can get the Internal Rate of Return (IRR) they are seeking. If you put $1 in a savings account today, you're lucky to get 1% interest. Investors want better returns, so they are willing to take more risk by buying companies. But, they want to be compensated for that risk. The rule of thumb in a healthy economy is that an investment in equities in the stock market returns 12%. Most buyers want a higher return than that, especially if they are using debt to help finance the purchase. If debt is expensive, then the desired rate of return must be higher to cover the cost of the debt. Many investors require at least a 20% return for tying up their money for 3 – 7 years in a business. Hence, they are looking for appreciation in the value of your company that only comes from growth and performance.

The Multiple will also indicate the rate of return the buyer wants. Paying '10 x EBITDA' for a company provides a 10% return based on the historical performance. Paying "5 x EBITDA" results in a 20% return. Most buyers acquire companies based on the idea that they are going to be able to realize greater returns than the company historically achieved.

Investors' Terms of Reference

Investors also look closely at the return on capital employed and the EBITDA as a percentage of the asset. For example, if a buyer purchases a company for $15 million in cash, returning profits (EBITDA) of $1.5million each year, it will deliver a 10% return on investment. If 50% of the $15million is financed, it will deliver approximately a 20% return. This is why some buyers, such as private equity groups, like to use debt to buy companies because it increases their internal rate of return. Debt allows them to invest less of their own capital.

Sophisticated investors also examine other factors, including how cash is generated, your assets and liabilities and how they contribute to the value of the firm, tangible assets (equipment and inventory), as well as intangible assets (intellectual property, client lists, distribution channels and brands). Professional valuators speculate on the outlook for the industry, your company's position in that industry, and the capital structure.

The next time you meet a friend for golf or a drink, and he or she says their cousin received offers of 7x, and they think that you would be a fool to settle for less, you must realize that your friend probably doesn't have all the facts. The company they're talking about might be in a very different business with different assets. You cannot compare the sale of companies and find meaningful evidence proving whether you have a good offer.

Instead, you must learn to use the investors' terms of reference and judge for yourself the facts that influence the EBITDA for your company. Remember, the value of your company will be affected by:

- the type of investor you are pursuing
- the method and criteria used in the investor's scorecard
- the industry in which you operate
- the certainty of future profitability
- the size of the market opportunity and how well your product/service fills a sizeable need
- the skill, capability, networks and goodwill that remain in the company to continue building and growing the company after you leave
- the need of the buyer and the subjective appraisal of 'fit' between buyer and seller
- similar or comparable deals if available

The value of your company will not be based on:

- your legacy
- your personal value to the company
- who you are

- what you've achieved
- what you think it's worth
- how much money you need to retire at the financial level you desire
- how well you get along with the prospective investor/buyer
- the value of someone else's deal
- how great your employees are

Your Reality Check

Ready to get your valuation reality check? Arming yourself with the truth about your company's value now will allow you to give yourself a BIG gift. If you know that you want a certain value for your company and you learn how to re-model your company so that it could be worth what you desire, then the probability that you can actually sell it will increase substantially.

How Investors Add and Subtract Value

Let's look deeper into how investors think. Investors look at your history; however, they are more interested in and, therefore, concerned with how easy it is to see the opportunities for a return moving forward.

You value the past.

Investors value the future profits, so they search out potential risks. This means that you need to stand in the investor's shoes and peer at your business from a detached perspective. Ask yourself, "If I had X amount of money to spend, would I buy this company if I wanted a better than average return on my investment?" Investors hope for more than 20% over three to five years.

Exploration Exercise #4
How Much is Your Firm Worth?

Use the following suggestions as a subjective guide to arrive at an estimate indicating how much your company might be worth, and to discover if there is operational work needed to help you get closer to your secret number. Investors use the term 'Enterprise Value' for 'company worth'. Related questions are in your PlayBook, so you can record your results and notes there.

- Look at your income statement for the last 12 months and find the <u>Earnings</u> before interest, tax, depreciation and amortization are deducted (EBITDA)

- Find the industry's typical EBITDA for your type of business (links supplied in the Appendix). How does your company rate against industry norms? Higher? Lower?

- Find your industry's current typical Multiple by buying the BizBuySell or BizMiner report for your geographic area (link in Appendix).

- Use the scorecard in the PlayBook to appraise your company from the buyer's perspective. Of course, this is a subjective exercise, but use your best guess.

- Take the Industry Multiple and multiply by the percentage you awarded your company. Multiply EBITDA by the reduced Multiple to find your estimated current enterprise value. Remember, this is not how professional valuators do this calculation. It is just an exercise that gives you a ballpark figure from which to work.

- Then calculate the potential enterprise value by multiplying your EBITDA by the Industry Multiple.

- Subtract the current value from the potential to determine the opportunity gap. By optimizing your company, you could take back some, or all, of the opportunity gap.

- Look at your financial statements for the last three years and run some of these calculations. For each 12-month period, calculate your firm's enterprise value to see how close you are to your target or secret number, and to uncover the size of the opportunity you gain from making your company attractive to investors.

	Example	This year	1 year ago	2 years ago	3 years ago
EBITDA	$3.0 m				
Industry Multiple	7 x				
Scorecard %	76%				
Estimated Multiple	5 x				
Estimated Current Enterprise Value	$15 m				
Potential Enterprise Value, if Optimized	$21 m				
Opportunity Gap	$6 m				
My Secret Number	$20 m				

Fig. 6

You should have a better idea of what your company is worth today, versus a couple of years ago.

Chapter 7 Summary

Learning to think like an investor allows you to see your company from a new perspective, as well as starting the letting go process. When you discover the reality of what your company is worth, you can now choose to improve the value or accept the value, and consider the options available to you based on this value.

This approach is in stark contrast to how many business owners conduct the biggest transaction of their lives. They expect a number that is unrealistic, and they haven't done the work to improve their organizations in order to justify that number. It makes for a very rocky road if the owner has an interested buyer, but can't negotiate a price that works for both parties. Disappointment is the result for everyone when the deal falls apart.

Now, you must decide whether you want to do the work of closing the gap between what your enterprise is worth today, and the amount for which you wish to sell the company. How much money do you want to leave on the table? In the next section, you will meet Vince and Paul and you'll learn what decisions they made when they learned what their company was worth.

Section IV
Step Two: Hone Goals and Decisions

"The problem with doing nothing is not knowing when you're finished."

Benjamin Franklin[23]

What you will learn in this section:

- What is important and unimportant to you
- How to decide whether you want to close the valuation gap
- What you have to do to make the decision and implement a plan to prepare for sale
- Important optimization goals

---

[23] Benjamin Franklin (17 January 1706 – 17 April 1890) was an American inventor, journalist, printer, diplomat and statesman

Chapter 8
What Saleability Story Do Your Numbers Predict?

What do I really want for myself? What do I really want for others? What do I really want for my relationships? Once you've asked yourself what you want, add one more question: How would I behave if I really wanted these results?

Kerry Patterson, Joseph Grenny,
Ron McMillan and Al Switzler[24]

What you will learn in this chapter:

- How to deal with the challenges standing in front of your exit goals
- What can block your ability to set useful and pragmatic goals
- What not to do when starting your exit journey
- How to get the sequence of goal-based activities in the right order so that you don't destabilize the operation
- Why putting the company's needs and goals in priority over your personal goals will actually increase the probability of your personal return

---

[24] Patterson, Kerry, Joseph Greeny, Ron McMillan, and Al Switzler. "Crucial Conversations: Tools for Talking When Stakes Are High" *McGraw-Hill* New York, NY 1976

Make the Right Decisions Before Taking Action

Vince and Paul, partners in VPA Mechanical Contracting, ran the numbers with their business consultant to get their reality-check using their current financial statements. They discovered their company was worth about $12.5 to $13.5 million, depending on the year reviewed. Taking a cool-eyed view of their operation with the help of their consultant, they finally understand why this valuation will not budge much past a 3.25x Multiple, given their current operational effectiveness and rollercoaster project-based revenue history.

Vince and Paul don't like the facts in front of them. It's clear to both of them that neither will get the exit they envision in their current state. So, they set their exit goal for an enterprise value of $18 million and made the decision to close the valuation gap by doing the required work. To achieve their goal, they need to increase their Multiple and their EBITDA. For Vince, the timing is not important, but Paul needs an end date, so they agree on four years.

What motivated these two owners to stop procrastinating and start making their future happen, was finding out that there were a limited number of buyers for mechanical contracting firms. Their potential investors were specific strategic buyers (other companies), but probably not financial buyers (private equity investors). Despite the $4.5 million gap in value, Vince and Paul wish to get out in four years, which means they have to face the following facts and create an action plan to change and improve their operation:

- **Fact:** They need to be acquired by a strategic buyer (a larger mechanical contractor) actively searching for a presence in their geographic market. Therefore, they need to conduct research to find which contractors are still acquiring, as well as undertake a serious appraisal of the future of commercial construction in their market area. If construction doesn't pick up soon, their company probably won't be saleable.

- **Fact:** Construction in their market is becoming active again. But, the economy won't give them the revenue growth it used to, so now they need to show growing gross margin despite less revenue. This will demonstrate to investors that they know how to manage their business effectively. To accomplish this they must find cash flow leaks, tighten processes and reduce actual variances against their project estimates. Vince and Paul always knew that they had variances between their estimates and actual project returns. But they always cheered their revenue numbers and winning new projects. They assumed that if they average a profit from all jobs, it was good enough to make money. Now, they know variance tracking is vital to their personal future, as well as the company's future. With coaching, they finally understand that to attract a buyer, they have to improve performance and reduce the risks investors care about. VPA needs to become a growing, cash flow steady going concern.

- **Fact:** Their ideal strategic buyer acquired only companies that earned the majority of revenue from services (steady cash flow), rather than bid projects. Vince and Paul only earned 20% of revenues from services and will have to build their value proposition on the service side, which means upgrading their 'side of the desk' attention to sales and hiring a sales person to acquire more service contracts.

- **Fact:** In order to sell, Vince and Paul will need to replace their positions in the company. They will need to afford to hire and train a new CEO, and either promote or hire a new operations whiz who will manage the project and service sides of the business. This will be a big financial investment, and it may mean taking a cut in what they take out of the company to make it work.

These are difficult facts to swallow, and each one is entangled in weighty issues unfamiliar to them. Yet, Vince and Paul are willing to listen, learn and deal with the reality of their situation, even if the news is difficult and the work challenging.

Start with the Conversation, Not the Action Plan

If you aren't thinking about and discussing your future with partners, advisors, or friends and family, chances are you aren't getting information to help map out a two-to-four year game plan or options.

Don't underestimate the enormity of feeling that such introspection or discussion causes. For some owners, the emotional impact of an uncertain future is enough to make them shelve the whole idea of an exit plan until 'later'. If you know your company's valuation doesn't meet your expectations, now is not the time to stop and wait; now it the time to choose your direction. Here are your options:

- Lower your financial expectations, but recognize you will still need to tune up the company. Or,

- Lower your financial expectations and don't do the tune up, realizing that your company will, most likely, be unable to find a buyer. Or,

- Keep your financial expectations and the kind of tune up that will make your company worth what you want and of great interest to several potential buyers. Waiting means inviting circumstances to eliminate your choices for you.

When you have a partnership, compound issues and colliding interests take root, and it's difficult to make a decision about which direction to take. If your communications are fuzzy, then the decision about how to sell a business can cause you to derail your game plan, as well as your partnership. You need to have numerous discussions with a wide variety of advisors, including a coach to help you gain clarity regarding your communications with each other. You need a game plan for whom to talk to, and when, so that you don't inadvertently do what Jenna and Rick did.

How Action Before Understanding Can Undermine Goals

Jenna and Rick Smith are in their late 50s and they travel the world selling Jenna's innovative spa and cosmetic products. It's a hectic life and they are rarely in the same city at the same time – they decide the pace is too hard on their marriage and they have had enough.

Rather than selling to the head offices of luxury resorts, they envision being together as *guests* of the luxury resorts. Hastily, between sales meetings and time zone changes, via phone, email and text, Jenna and Rick cobble together a solution for their problem. They conclude that a management buyout will suit them perfectly and, the next time they are both in their own HQ, they will pitch it to Frank, their Chief Operating Officer.

Frank steers the Smith Spa Products (SSP) and he enacts the plans Jenna and Rick envision, as well as oversees the manufacturing of their products. Jenna and Rick are their company's product innovators and chief business development stars. Frank is the stabilizing third leg in their business.

It's Monday. Jenna won't let their jet lag stop them from getting to the office early. Thinking Frank will approve of this opportunity to buy SSP from them, Jenna proceeds to their office with excitement for all parties concerned. They stop in at Frank's office just as he is looking through last month's financial statements.

He puts the file in front of Jenna.

Jenna closes it and puts it aside rather than glancing at the highlighted numbers. Five minutes later, Frank is leaning back in his office chair in silence. Jenna's enthusiasm for her pitch isn't having the effect she had planned. She looks at Rick.

While Frank has wondered about having his own company one day, he doesn't consider himself an entrepreneur. He is their employee, not their partner. Privately, he describes his role at SSP to friends, by saying "I am risk averse, which creates a good check and balance with Jenna and Rick, who are risk takers."

Normally, when Jenna or Rick are in the office, Frank will discuss how to deliver on their promises they have made to their customers and how to meet deadlines; but, now it seems to Frank that they also have the company's entire future weighing them down. Frank now knows his bosses want out. Does he want in?

He stares at the numbers he highlighted in the financial statement.

The Habit of Taking Action Before Getting Informed

The typical North American entrepreneur is a risk taker, working off the gut, sure in every decision, keeping an eye on the prize and a firm hand on the wheel. But, for every strength there is a weakness, and taking action before understanding the nature of the problem, as well as the potential impacts of that action on an organization, are the entrepreneur's blind sides.

Jenna and Rick enacted a plan with their personal hats on, without understanding what needs attention for the health of the company – i.e., when they should wear their functional hats, so that the company's needs take priority over personal needs. By enacting this ill-informed plan, they jeopardize a key working relationship and now they're feeling the unexpected ramifications of their actions.

Jenna isn't getting the response she expects, so Jenna passes the ball to Rick. In full sales mode, Rick thinks all he has to do is persuade Frank to accept their plan, and he puts their cards on the table. He begins to illustrate all the benefits Frank would accrue from owning their firm, pushing a shareholder hat onto Frank's furrowed brow. Then he caps off the pitch by disclosing their secret number. For $8 million, the company can be Frank's.

Only then do Rick and Jenna finally hear a response from their trusted star employee. Without much more comment, he suggests they should get a professional valuation before further discussion. Thinking they heard a buy signal, Jenna and Rick agree and set the ball in motion.

While that might seem like a logical next step, it isn't a worthwhile investment until the parties actually determine that Frank is interested and financially able, and that the company can remain operational without Rick and Jenna in their functional roles.

By 11:00 AM, Jenna has called a major accounting firm to initiate the valuation process. And, Frank, in his role of COO, is supplying the documents, financial statements and forecasts. In fact, Frank should already have a good idea about the true enterprise value.

By conducting the conversation with Frank, Jenna and Rick created instability in their relationship with a critical employee, shared a potentially unrealistic enterprise value, and saddled Frank with the expectation that he should be grateful for the opportunity. This situation is highly distracting to the operation. The company's needs should remain the first priority. But Jenna and Rick are thinking with their shareholders' hats and, typically, expect Frank to wear the functional hat. Now he, too, is expected to think like a shareholder. Who is looking out for the company's best interests? Furthermore, an expensive valuation will be based on the earnings history, which has little bearing on the future of the firm without its primary product development and sales team.

Therefore, the valuation will be of little use to guide the management buyout discussion other than for Frank to 'prove' the company is not worth what Jenna and Rick want from him. The company is now in jeopardy. Six weeks later, Jenna and Rick (still wearing their shareholder hats) are sitting in a hushed boardroom staring at a number at the bottom of the heavy paper that reflects half of their secret number. They don't understand how the accounting firm came to the conclusion their company is only worth $4 million, half of their exit dream number, nor do they understand the Multiple number. Rather than asking questions, Rick starts to dispute it. He gets defensive about how the accounting firm performed the work, and Jenna suspects Frank of not presenting company information in the best light.

Jenna and Rick have no grounding in what buyers seek or what affects their perception of value. If they are not willing to understand and learn how an investor perceives value, then they give themselves no opportunity to understand what it might take to make the company worth their secret number of $8 million. They leave the boardroom fuming, not to mention they're $15,000 poorer.

If you were in Frank's shoes, what would you think of Jenna's 'generous' offer? Even more challenging is that while Frank might be interested in acquiring SSP, and he may think he can negotiate with Jenna and Rick to arrive at a mutually beneficial value, he has no immediate means of funding such a transaction. It can take years for a management buyout to be structured in such a way that it can work financially for a salaried employee.

Jenna and Rick have used their short time frame as the driving force for pushing an ill thought out solution. If they want out fast, and with the full purchase price, then a management buyout would be the last option on the list unless Frank has immediate access to capital. These events are happening quickly because that's the way Jenna and Rick like to do things – multi-tasking and winging it based on scant information and gut instinct. But, the pace and lack of preparation means Frank will be unable to make any offer, even if he has any interest.

Jenna and Rick now have several problems because they started with action before they conducted research, explored all of the company's needs with the right hat on, did not engage in conversations to gain an education about their options, and didn't have the right action plan. Their first problem is they may lose their star employee due to the conflict and mistrust that has built up over the valuation. Not having an experienced COO may threaten the company's future, and the possibility exists that Jenna or Rick will have to take over the operational and financial reins. It's too bad neither of them have strength in those areas of operations.

What Jenna and Rick didn't know about preparing a company for sale is killing their potential to realize *any* sale. And, even more troublesome is the Multiple used to calculate the enterprise value of the company was based on the management team already in place. If Frank were to leave, the Multiple applied will be considerably lower, thereby making their company worth even less because of Frank's departure.

Their retirement and exit dream have moved farther into the distant future – not closer, as they anticipated.

Take Steps in the Right Order

Don't get attached to a secret number without knowing if you can realize it in the timeframe or method you think will work, and without getting an independent third party to assess the company's current state. A valuator may be able to tell you what contributes and detracts from the Multiple, but not how to optimize your company to improve your Multiple.

Jenna and Rick could have groomed SSP to be attractive to the type of investor that might have paid a premium for their formulations, designs and client list. But, instead, they fixated on getting out fast and selling it to the first person they thought may be interested and at the number they wanted. They also tried to skip steps crucial to make the sale happen.

One year later, the mistrust and resentment that occurred caused Frank to leave the company. Their most trusted employee is gone, taking with him his operational and financial knowledge. Rick is now on the road alone, and Jenna is trying to run operations and develop products herself.

She hired an accountant.

They now know they need to continue working for the foreseeable future to rebuild it and then grow the company.

> The best strategy for a company where the owner creates the intellectual property and product is to plan to be acquired by a competitor who has the talent, but needs the distribution channel and new formulations to complement their existing products.

The fact remains that this was a blunder on many levels. If Jenna and Rick were to attempt to sell the company, who would be in charge of product development and take over sales in an industry where strong relationships dictate future sales once they exit the company? It could never have been Frank, even if he were willing and able to buy the company. Jenna's product development skills and Rick's sales relationships are too pivotal to their company's future, and this predicament, over and above any other problems, makes this company un-saleable.

You Have to be Replaceable

If you didn't fully grasp that you must replace your functional role (depending on the type of acquirer you select), or at least step back from day-to-day operations for at least a year before you sell (not after), Jenna and Rick's story may make this much clearer.

The best strategy for a company where the owner creates the intellectual property and products is to plan to be acquired by a competitor who already has the product development talent, but needs the distribution channel and new formulations to complement their existing products. By following our Action Blueprint, you won't make the same mistakes Jenna and Rick made.

If moving out of the way in the next few months rather than two to three years from now is not palatable or affordable, then you may want to acquire a much better understanding of what you really want, and measure that against the reality of your situation. You can't sell a company that requires you to run it, unless you want to stay on and work for the new owners in the same capacity. Only specific types of buyers see this arrangement as beneficial and it often doesn't last very long, because it becomes very uncomfortable for the autonomy-loving entrepreneur to report to a new boss.

It's difficult to trust anyone to take over if you don't have criteria and a plan. If you think no one can manage things as well as you, you need to learn to:

- Change your mindset and decide to solve the problem
- Set aside the funds to pay for your replacement(s)
- Define the role, responsibility and authority of the roles you currently serve
- Learn how to hire people with critical skills for each role
- Train and mentor them properly
- Learn how to delegate effectively
- Transition key internal and external relationships to the new hires
- Trust that you selected the right people and that they are capable to do the job

133

If you have partners like Vince and Paul do in Chapter 2, how can you start a conversation based on relevant and crucial information in order to build a sound plan, so you can all be on the same page?

The Foundation of a Successful Exit Plan

Take a page out of Vince and Paul's epic journey to their exit – mechanical contracting is a hard-scramble industry and business owners wrestle to keep the margins in positive territory on every job. It's the kind of cash flow, rollercoaster business that most investors see as risk heavy and, therefore, a poor investment.

Vince and Paul are both tough, take charge, hard-nosed guys. Vince is in his mid-fifties, and Paul hasn't met the end of his fourth decade, but he feels like he's twenty years older. Before their exit discussion, they used to both talk of passing the company to their kids and hanging out at their cabins or fishing. In fact, several family members worked at VPA, so it actually seemed like a nice idea.

One day, John, Vince's best friend, took him aside and suggested he plan his exit strategy just as he did when he took on a new project.

Vince tried to avoid the topic by cracking a joke, but his friend persisted. In the end, John helped Vince summarize what he really needed in terms of an exit date, and a date to end the struggle to manage VPA profitability.

John brought up the idea of giving VPA to Vince's kids and asked if either of them had done anything to learn the business. What about Paul's cousins who also worked at VPA? Then he asked Vince if he would hire any of them to be his replacement.

Vince winced. In truth, his kids had worked summers in the company, but neither showed aptitude for estimating, project management or contracting. And, while Paul's cousins were crackerjacks in the field, they knew nothing about managing a company. Vince's reality check was just beginning, thanks to his best friend and, as a result, he was able to bring up the difficult subject with his partner, Paul.

Paul listened and nodded, knowing that Vince likes to talk about changes, but often lacks the follow through to plan and enact those changes. Paul went along with the exit idea to keep the peace in the office, but, much to his surprise, Vince did follow John's advice and found an advisor to come in and talk to them about their future. When the two of them finally sat down with the experienced facilitator for their first conversation, they found the courage to reveal their concerns by learning how to say to each other what they couldn't voice previously.

Vince wanted to grow before they sold, through acquisitions. But, Paul admitted to Vince that it was all he could do to get up on Monday mornings and that he could hardly wait to get out at 4:30 P.M. Paul didn't want to be doing this much longer.

Vince was shocked by what he heard. For some business partners, this type of conversation would hang in the air and not go any further. Avoiding conflict was Paul's biggest priority and he worked hard to steer clear of Vince's demands day in and day out.

The conversation did not break down at that point because they had a capable advisor/facilitator. This was a chance to keep talking and work through what each of them wanted, even though their needs and concerns were as similar as summer and winter. Most partners rarely enter into this kind of discussion for fear that one of them will angrily leave. But, Vince and Paul knew where that road would take them. They stayed in the room, learned how to discuss their concerns in a non-threatening and non-judgemental way and, as a result, learned more about each other's interests and struggles than they had in twenty years of being in business.

In fact, they did more than just swap stories; they got serious about what they wanted to do with the company and their lives.

Despite different time horizons, different needs, different concerns and twenty years' worth of gripes about each other, they agreed on a number they wanted the company to be worth in four years, learned what work was needed in order to shift the business, and they agreed to work on dealing with Paul's frustrations.

These two tough guys with strong personalities beat their typical tendency to argue and found a way to hear each other by being open and honest, and learned which hat to wear depending on the topic of conversation. They learned how to set context for their ideas, ask good questions and reframe what they heard from each other until each felt understood.

Remember the acquisitions Vince wanted to do? When Paul learned they needed them for higher service revenues, he saw the purpose in acquiring companies with contracts in new service areas. In addition, he saw how to make their company valuable to larger mechanical contractors wanting to get into their geographic territory. They felt inspired and rejuvenated by their new goals!

The biggest lesson they learned was that assets and processes don't run companies – people do. Improving the company's project performance would come only through transparent and real information exchange essential for reducing the variance number to increase gross margins. That will change the atmosphere in their company from one in which the employees are too intimidated to talk to either partner, to one where people feel respected for sharing their views and ideas for improvements.

And, along the way, Paul found talents and strengths he never knew he had when he reformed how their people manage their project systems through motivating employees by mentoring them. These positive changes came about because they committed to communicate effectively and then led by example. As a result, employees started to reveal strengths neither Paul nor Vince had noticed. And, VPA reaped the benefits!

Can you see yourself having these types of open and reflective conversations with your partners and family to build and enact your exit blueprint?

Chapter 8 Summary

There are many aspects to an exit strategy. If you have partners, you must harmonize and adjust their needs, your needs and the needs of the company in order to suit the *reality* of what your organization needs. You must wear your functional hat to evaluate what's best for the company as the top priority.

Making the company's requirements for a healthy future a priority over the needs of any or all shareholders is the sound way to an orderly, low-risk and more probable exit. Then you need to gain all shareholders' agreement to buy into and commit to working through the systemic issues to ensure you activate the optimization plan.

One of the biggest barriers an owner can inadvertently encounter is to create an action plan in a hurry. You will create the best plan after gaining a clear understanding of what you need and what you can accomplish. Do not make your rush to an exit the primary driver for developing your succession solution.

Chapter 9
Knowing What You Really Want – and, Need

"It is more important to know where you are going than to get there quickly. Do not mistake activity for achievement."

Mabel Newcomer[25]

What you will learn in this chapter:

- How to be clear about what is important to you
- How the act of being intentional can clear away unwanted thinking habits to gain clarity
- The activities involved in the five phases of an exit

After reading these stories, is it clear what you really want? Perhaps you're not sure because, like many people, you may be unable to articulate what you really want because you aren't thinking in those terms. It's often true that we know more about what we don't want. Paul didn't want to make acquisitions. He didn't want to deal with the conflict he *thought* they would bring into an already conflict-ridden daily grind. But, thinking about what you don't want leads to more of 'what you don't want', not new and empowering solutions. Instead, *find out what is important to you and your partners* and move toward what you do want,

---

[25] Mabel Newcomer 1892 – 1983 was a Professor of Economics at Vassar University and a tax expert.

thereby keeping you focused and on track when the going gets tough.

The one thing that you don't want on the path toward your goal is a situation highly charged with emotion, such as fear of uncertainty. It can happen if you think, "I might not be able to sell my company," or, "I might not get the price I want," or, "I might not like retirement, so why bother," or, 'My partner won't change, so why try and talk to him or her?" These cynical or resigned thoughts tend to block the mind and keep it from thoughtful and purposeful ideas. The idea is not to block emotion, but to use the tools discussed in Chapter 3, Demystifying Challenges, to reframe negative thoughts or doubting questions into positive thoughts or questions that keep your mind on your needs and a well-planned exit.

Using the reframing tool when those thoughts creep into your mind will help manage the urge to push it all away, and to not deal with anything related to selling or the future. You want to acknowledge the emotional impact of your next steps and keep moving forward, rather than expend effort to quell the emotional ramifications of this very major life step. Reframing the doubt and talking to people you trust accomplishes your goal.

But, as we have seen, the opposite approach won't serve you, either. When you are too optimistic with thoughts of realizing that secret number, and being retired with money to burn and time to do anything (just like Jenna and Rick), you tend to ignore critical information if you think it will affect your dream. Again, reframing, discussing with trusted people and learning all you can about the exit and optimization process is your best starting point in your action plan.

So as you can see, neither negative nor positive imagery will give you a true idea of what you really want because it's not yet in the realm of your experience. If you haven't lived it, even the possibility of something not yet experienced can be viewed as 'probably not possible' and, therefore, it's impossible in your mind. To extricate yourself from this tangled, polarized thinking and get yourself on track to a possible future, stop the debate and simply make the decision to pursue the desired result you really want.

It's a very powerful act!

To help you better articulate what you really want, here is a list of desired outcomes most business owners wish to accomplish:

- Knowledge and guidance to transfer your business, without too much hassle, into the hands of the next buyer

- A game plan to get you from today to the day the check goes into your bank account

- Peace of mind knowing that you have passed on your legacy to capable hands for the betterment of your employees, stakeholders, customers, and the community

- The freedom from time constraints and worry to follow inspiration and motivation to whatever excites you for your next act in life

- Enough money to make the years of investment and sacrifice worth it

If you can think of other points, feel free to add them to this list in your PlayBook and then keep them within sight. If you do nothing other than follow these aspirational goals, you will be well on your way to achieving them. We call learning to focus on what you really want, rather than on doubts, irritants, and frustrations 'being intentional'.

How to Work Intentionally

To acquire this powerful skill of being intentional, you need to change your internal dialog. To maintain intentionality, you must interrupt any thinking patterns that stray to negative scenarios, especially if you tend toward cynicism.

Do not awaken your cynicism!

Your energy and appetite for making changes is deeply affected by the quality and tone of your internal dialogue. Cynicism might be satisfying in the moment, but it can rot your ability to achieve the future you really want. By indulging cynicism, you remove your ability to motivate yourself and others to change. Cynicism blocks thoughts of hope and, therefore, action. Reframe what you think, say and do toward what you want to achieve. Then, it will stop sapping your energy, ideas and organizational relationships.

Working intentionally also continues to do its magic when you engage in other types of conversations. If you're the sole owner, then break your pattern of going it alone and talk to your spouse, or, perhaps, your adult children or best friend. Share your thoughts with those close to you who have the ability to draw out of you what is important, like Vince's friend, John, did for him. Allow yourself to get this help so you can order your thinking into an appropriate action plan.

The point is that owners need someone to talk to whom they trust. Hearing yourself give voice to thoughts and concerns you haven't taken the time to explore, gives you greater clarity about what is critical to you. A discussion promotes new ideas and allows for exploration into how to achieve your goals and deal with concerns, potential roadblocks and frustrations.

Even if your exit date is ten or fifteen years off, the best gift you can give your family and stakeholders is to put an exit date on the calendar and start working toward that goal. In addition to talking to family and friends, look for a business advisor and coach to work with, so you don't put your company at risk, as Jenna and Rick did with their hasty plan. If you have these conversations, you'll also begin to demystify your profitability problem.

Remember – don't limit your conversations to one source. There are many people in your life that you can talk to as you plan this exciting journey. Choose people who will support you in setting personal goals, and share your experiences with them as events unfold. As a result, your exit will be much more rewarding!

The Phases of an Exit

Now that we have zeroed in on your internal processes, it will be useful to pull back out and give you a 'big picture overview' of the five phases of the exit process. Your action blueprint prepares you and your company to begin Phase One, and it sets you up to start Phase Two.

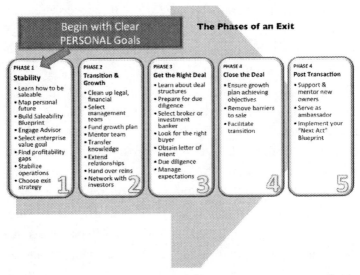

Fig. 7

Phase One – Stability

- Learn & discuss future with partners
- Build your Saleability Blueprint
- Acquire a business advisor to help you lead change
- Select enterprise value goal
- Find profitability gaps
- Stabilize operations
- Choose exit strategy
- Develop personal succession plan

Once you set your personal goals, make agreements with any partners or family, and make the decision to invest in closing the gap between your enterprise value and your secret number, it's time to learn about stabilization. To stabilize your operations means to optimize all resources, so the company functions effectively. Most companies grow somewhat haphazardly, and this is evident if your company tries to grow and, instead, experiences expansion and contraction cycles. Contraction will occur when internal systems and processes that allow employees and managers to share and hand off critical information are missing. In addition, contraction happens when there are missing indicators regarding how activities are contributing to or crippling the business. The work of stability is to maintain consistency in all areas, so that all departments function well together, thereby resulting in profitability. Once your company is stable, steady growth is possible *without* contraction, and then your firm will be attractive to investors. Achieving stability can take six to eighteen months.

Phase Two – Transition & Growth

- Develop growth plan
- Work with lender to fund growth
- Select management team
- Mentor team
- Transfer knowledge
- Extend relationships
- Hand over the reins
- Network with investors
- Clean up legal agreements and financial reporting

Your next task is to mentor your people and transition the company toward the day when you are not there daily. This means you must teach your employees what you know, and make it easy for them to build relationships with critical people in your marketplace. Simultaneously, you may wish to lure a senior manager to take over the leadership of the company in order to keep it healthy and to help it grow. Your hard work of stabilizing the company requires a different skill set than the leadership and management for healthy balanced growth. So, find a leader who knows your industry with the experience in growing a company to the size required to match your enterprise value goal. Then, spend the next year mentoring that person while networking with ideal acquirers and building your exit advisory team. If your ideal acquirer involves being bought out by employees, start meeting with advisors now to learn how this might work and whether employees might work with an M&A lawyer, in order to check agreements for any deal breaker problems long before you start looking for a buyer. Get an audit on financial statements. Clean personal expenses off the books.

Phase Three – the Exit

- Learn about deal structures
- Prepare for due diligence
- Select broker or investment banker
- Look for the right buyer
- Obtain Letter of Intent
- Due diligence

If your desired acquirer is a financial or strategic buyer, then this is the stage when you need a team of advisors to help you learn about and put your deal in place. Advisors include an intermediary, your M&A lawyer and accounting team to take care of you and your interests from the point of preparing for the search through the time of first contact (regarding a potential purchase) with the ideal acquirer, to the day after the deal closes.

Phase Four – Close the Deal

- Remove barriers
- Facilitate transition

Don't fool yourself into thinking that you will finalize the deal quickly and easily, even if you have the perfect company that achieved operational effectiveness and worked through the management transition well. The truth is that most acquirers surround themselves with advisors, and they actively search for risk points, which can be quite stressful on owners. So, aiming toward a closing is like trying to hit a moving target. Due diligence consumes much of your time, and your attitude through this process must be helpful, confident and transparent. Not only that, your company must hit forecasted performance targets despite these distractions. You also will be conducting due diligence under wraps, keeping your intentions from employees, in an effort not to incite uncertainty and fear, thereby ruining productivity. A lot can go wrong in this phase and only your will and your professionalism can keep the deal on track.

Phase Five – Post Transaction

- Support & mentor new owners
- Serve as ambassador
- Implement your "Next Act" Blueprint

Many deals today have earn-out provisions, which mean you are unlikely to get your entire purchase price upfront and in cash. Many acquirers expect owners to 'prove their growth plans' and it's common to pay out the purchase price over two to three years, depending on whether or not you meet performance targets. If you sell to a manager or family member, you will, most likely, be paid over time because of the limits of their ability to finance the deal. You are tied to the future performance of your company, without you at the helm. Your job during the earn-out period is to continue to serve as a mentor, ambassador, coach, sales person, networker and all-around helpful person to ensure that the team you are leaving behind has what it needs to meet its mark.

It should be apparent that preparing for sale will require investing in activities and strategies that you may tend to avoid, in order to ensure a better return for shareholders. Therefore, you need to be clear when setting goals that you are willing to:

- Obtain and use advice (business, tax, legal, financial, organizational, personal)
- Recruit experienced management

- Upgrade financial systems
- Invest in operational upgrades
- Lead change to increase operational effectiveness and efficiency

Chapter 9 Summary

The work of becoming intentional may require you to adapt long-used thinking habits by using the reframing tool to discover what is important to you. Learning to be intentional is vital to manage the emotional effects of this transition, and it will also be an important mentoring skill that you will want to use in order to help lead your employees through the changes. Change often surfaces people's negative thoughts, and reframing helps them to find and focus on what is important to them, so they can build a sound plan.

There are five phases to an exit process, and the four-step action blueprint prepares you to step into Phases One and Two.

Section V
Step Three: Hunt the Right Acquirer

Making your mark on the world is tough. If it were easy, everybody would do it. But it's not. It takes patience and commitment, and it comes with plenty of failure along the way. The real test is not whether you avoid this failure, because you won't. It's whether you let it harden or shame you into inaction, or whether you learn from it. Whether you choose to persevere.

Barack Obama[26]

What you will learn in this section:

- Types of Advisors
- Types of Buyers and what is important to them
- The work of attracting the right Buyers

---

[26] Obama, Barack. From a speech delivered in 2006 to the Campus Progress Conference.

Chapter 10
Who Helps Owners Sell a Business?

"We are drowning in information, but starved for knowledge."
John Naisbitt[27]

What you will learn in this chapter:

- Types of advisors you will want to work with for each size of business
- What to do if your company might not be saleable
- What buyers look for when considering an acquisition

The first advisor you will want to work with is an exit-planning consultant. This expert is skilled at the personal, interpersonal and operational needs of the entire exit process, so make sure the person you select has this broad-based holistic approach. You may also want to work with a personal life coach at this time to help you make mindset changes and explore options for your future or deal with current conflicts.

Your exit-planning consultant should be able to help you work through the stability issues. We present a number of solutions for typical stability problems in the Helm the Transition section. You

---

[27] Naisbitt, John and Patricia Aburdene "Megatrends 2000" *Avon Books, New York, NY* 1990.

can find a directory for Exit-Planning Consultants in the Appendix.

Your next step is to work with a financial management expert who can make sense of your financial results and reveal opportunities and areas that need attention. You will want your accountant to do an audit to make sure your company's books are sound.

Then, you will want to seek a lawyer who is skilled in the M&A process in order to complete a thorough scouring of all of your agreements, as well as fix any that will prevent or restrict a change in ownership. This is also the time to revise shareholder agreements and straighten out any misconceptions among shareholders.

While working with the lawyer, you will also want to meet with wealth management and tax advisors who can advise you on the best tax strategies, company structure and personal wealth management.

Invest in advisors and this restructuring at least two years before your exit date to make sure the right things are in place to protect you and the company legally and financially.

Throughout this process, ask many questions about why your advisors are recommending each action, so you keep yourself on the learning curve, thereby enabling yourself to see your company as an investor would.

Three types of agents who represent a business throughout the sale process are:

- Business brokers
- Mergers and Acquisition (M&A) advisors
- Investment bankers.

The type of agent you select to work with depends on the size of the business. Business brokers work with businesses under $5 million, and, typically, they take a 10% success fee with no upfront fee.

Business owners in the mid-size category (such as we are discussing in this book) will work with M&A advisors. These firms know how to attract professional investors and financial buyers, such as private equity groups or strategic buyers, and other companies in your industry. Or, your competitors. They can sometimes create other alternatives to help you extract your retirement wealth. M&A advisors will charge you a retainer or consulting fee up front, and they will assist with financing alternatives. They will also charge a success fee built on a sliding scale that declines with purchase price.

Investment bankers usually work with public and private businesses worth $40 million and up. M&A advisors and investment bankers sometimes compete for the same mid-market businesses in hot industries.

Is there ever a time when you can take on the sale of your organization yourself without using an intermediary or agent? If you are selling to an already identified potential partner, then you may need to work only with an M&A attorney and a tax accountant. If you haven't found that desired partner, a broker may be able to help you find the right kind of partner. They work on the 'buy side' as well as the 'sell side'.

The more important question is this: if you have never sold a business before, do you want to take this opportunity to invest the time to learn how to do it effectively in order to find a buyer? For some owners, they identify the buyer, the type of deal is straight forward, and all they need is the guidance from legal and tax advisors. Know how much time you can invest, what your strengths are and whether you are inclined to learn what you don't know in order to find the right buyer and prepare a deal that will work for all parties.

When you use an intermediary, you are buying into their network of relationships, which is similar to the multiple listing services a realtor uses . . . it's too bad that these listing services don't exist for the buying and selling of businesses. The marketing of a business is very different. The right intermediary for you knows who is looking for the kind of business that you are selling, and why. This knowledge should shorten the time between the day you are ready to sell and the moment you discover a willing buyer.

Selling the Smaller Company

You may be able to sell your smaller company depending on the benefit your business might bring to a future owner. For example, think about younger entrepreneurs, recent business immigrants or people who lose or are laid off from their jobs as your potential exit partners. There are business brokers who specialize in making these kinds of connections.

A potential buyer wanting to 'buy a job' will be looking for some or all of these attributes:

- A company financial picture that provides a good living for the foreseeable future
- Obvious potential to grow to the next level
- Help from you to become acclimated to the business and its key relationships
- Room for improvement, so they can put their own stamp on the operation

If your company can provide these opportunities, then your business might be transferrable or saleable to a current or new business partner, or even an employee who can gain access to financing in concert with being rewarded with dividends from your company to aid the exit process. If this option makes sense for the size and position of your operation, then your next step is to improve your operation so there is room for this new partner, financially and operationally, and then work through a business broker who specializes in businesses of your size to find a partner.

Take-Over by a Family Member

As we mentioned previously, never gift the company to family. This is a recipe for wealth destruction and family heartache, and the statistics bear this out. However, do _sell_ the company to any family member who is willing and able to obtain financing and effectively lead the company.

Structure this type of deal in the same way you would structure a sale to an employee. Use advisors (business, tax, legal, acquisition). Additionally, make sure you optimize your company for profitability, and that your successor can perform successfully before you finalize the sale. When someone has a stake in the company, the company does well. Even with this type of business transfer, don't neglect following the saleability blueprint you will develop to ensure your new owner learns how to make decisions for the company by wearing the right hat. Family business owners often struggle by wearing the functional hat rather than their shareholder hat most of the time.

Making Money in a Tough Market

Many businesses are facing a challenging future with an economy that is uncertain. Remember, optimized companies can make money in any economy. That can be hard to think about if your time window closed and the 'Freedom at 55' dream is dead. Know that deals are happening with some companies, especially those that are improved to be attractive to investors. The secret is to be willing to learn what doesn't contribute to your bottom line and make the right changes to offer products and services that are profitable.

If your company is struggling and it isn't in saleable condition, relax. This doesn't mean you will be stuck working into your sixties and seventies unless you want to. Even during a recession or slow economic growth, profitability, high performance, and even growth in market share is, indeed, possible – *if* you arm yourself with the education, planning and optimization.

If you are unsatisfied with current returns, don't let a soft market and the media deter you from taking these actions. Your employees will enjoy a better working environment, your customers will get an improved set of solutions, and your community will benefit from your business, all of which contribute important parts of its economic rejuvenation. By choosing to optimize your company, you, as the primary investor, will be able to give yourself the same high rate of return a buyer will expect. Check out the chapters on Helming the Transition for recommendations on where and how to start.

The decisions you make today to build an action blueprint and then implement it over the next two or ten years, will help your bottom line and help you position for an exit when the time is right. You will also give yourself more time to perform the stabilization and growth plan, which is a very good thing!

What if the Company isn't Saleable?

If you can't say your company is poised and able to grow, and you admit it's a struggle to give yourself a regular paycheck, then you need to learn how to make your business more profitable and, therefore, attractive to a potential buyer. Hire a business coach to review your operation and help you improve the areas that contribute to your less-than-ideal performance.

You will find many ideas for the typical issues that businesses face in the final chapters of the book.

If you are not in a position to invest further time and energy, then look seriously at winding down your operation and get what you can from the sale of your assets. Waiting for a buyer who may never come is not a good environment for you, your employees or your customers. If your business isn't profitable, it's an indication that your company needs changes and, without intentionally making those substantial changes to the operation, product or solution, your investment is wasting away rather than making you a good return.

Compare your return on investment with the return you would get investing the same amount into real estate or even a certificate of deposit. If your business is not appreciating, and you are too dispirited or not interested in making improvements, you may be better off winding it down and spending your resources and energy on something that better suits you and your investments goals.

Chapter 10 Summary

Regarding most transition transactions, you will need an agent as well as legal, financial and probably business advice to achieve a sale. Even if your business is smaller, there are still options for transitioning ownership. If the business isn't saleable, the best solution after evaluating the investment is to wind it down.

Chapter 11
What Buyers Search for in an Acquisition

"There are three ways of dealing with difference: domination, compromise, and integration. By domination only one side gets what it wants; by compromise neither side gets what it wants; by integration we find a way by which both sides may get what they wish."

Mary Parker Follett[28]

In this chapter, you will learn:

- Types of exit options
- The four types of buyers
- How they make acquisitions
- Current deal statistics
- How buyers perceive value and risk

For a business owner, there are four methods to achieve an exit:

✓ Go Public

✓ Sell to new or existing partners

---

[28] Follett, Mary Parker, Henry C. Metcalf and L. Urwick. "Dynamic Administration: The Collected Papers of Mary Parker Follett" *Harper & Brothers, Publishers.*, 1940, p. 31-32.

✓ Be acquired by another company
✓ Sell to a financial group

Going Public

Currently, due to increasingly stringent regulations, going public has become an onerous endeavor, which only gets more distracting and formidable after the enterprise becomes public. For this reason, we think it's best to leave this topic to the books that cover it in depth, as well as to the legal experts. If going public is something from which you think your firm will benefit, discuss it with a securities specialist to learn about the pros and cons.

Selling to or Taking on Partners

If current partners or employees become interested in buying out your share, begin a discussion of your available options with a specialist in employee buyouts or employee share ownership plans (ESOP). See Appendix for resources.

Being Acquired

A 'professional acquirer' refers to a financial buyer, such as a private equity group or a strategic buyer (one company buying another company). These buyers choose to acquire a company for many reasons, and the two most prominent reasons are for financial return and strategic entry.

Buyers are investors first – they are mostly interested in enjoying a return on their invested capital, which means that the amount of interest they have in your business relates directly to the amount of profit they think it can earn once they own it.

The Four Types of Buyers

Generally, beyond financial returns, each buyer is interested in something specific about a business, a certain industry, size or type of company.

1. **Management Buyout (MBO)**: when your employees, key manager(s) or a family member wants to buy the company and run it. They are interested in job security. To accomplish an MBO requires a company with steady and significant cash flow to pay out the exiting owner who is willing to receive that pay out over an extended period of time. A variation of this is the Employee Stock Ownership Plan (ESOP).

2. An **individual**: like you, who wants to 'buy a job and a nice little business'. Each is interested in learning the business from exiting owner.

3. A **Strategic Buyer**: generally another company who wants your company because of a perceived strategic advantage it will provide. They are interested in your company's key clients, distribution in a market they need to access, and/or products or intellectual property that add value to their offerings. They look for synergies between your company and theirs that will reduce operational costs and increase sales volume.

4. A **Financial Buyer** or **Private Equity Group (PEG)**: a limited partnership of individuals entrusted to acquire companies for strong cash flow and return on investment on behalf of a group of funding sources. They are interested in companies with high growth potential and strong predictable cash flow. They seek loyal customers and those under long-term contracts.

Which Acquirer is the Right Buyer for Your Company?

Finding the Right Buyer

Employees/ESOP: There are 11,500 Employee Stock Ownership Plans in the US. The number is not increasing. A few are done each year, but they are complex in nature. Refer to the Appendix for information on the ESOP Association.

MBO: Do some research. Talk to consultants or mercantile banks that specialize in structuring MBOs, as well as your bank (for debt options) to get an opinion as to whether this is an alternative for you, given your time window and the company's ability to generate cash flow. You will want an M&A advisor to help you find the right financing. Know what it will take for a deal to happen before presenting any plans or ideas to your staff. Your ability (and, your chosen successor's ability) to steer the company from the steady operation it is today to a growth machine able to churn out significant cash flow, is necessary and vital to fund those dividend payments, whether for arm's length transactions or an MBO with family members.

New Partner: You will need to be sure you are the type of person who can work collaboratively with someone, mentor them, trust them and share knowledge as you set them up for success. If you've been a lone wolf, chances are this option is not for you. This also holds true for working with a family member.

If you are considering bringing in new partners that you don't know, it may be best to think about a staged integration plan that culminates in the purchase of your shares. This type of buyer might emerge from a pool of management level hiring candidates, your business network, a business broker, an immigration attorney specializing in investor visas, or even a friend or neighbor. Think of finding that perfect partner the same way you would look for and screen a new general manager or vice president. Write a job description, map out responsibilities, include the role in the organizational chart and set expectations for performance.

The right person will have a similar vision for earning their way into an ownership position. You are going to be married to this person for the next few years, so hire them with the idea that if the arrangement works, you will set up an earn-out to transfer ownership. If you're thinking of a family member for the job, make sure they qualify in comparison to other external candidates.

A good first step to test out the compatibility and ability of the partnership is to consider profit sharing rather than ownership. That way, if things don't work out, it's easier to end the arrangement. If you can, solidify the partnership then develop an earn-out agreement. Sketch out the game plan at the outset, decide on a target date for a joint performance review (you both have to evaluate the situation), and set up milestone and performance targets (even for family members).

One of the largest, untapped markets for potential new partners or buyout partners is recent immigrants.[29] They bring their wealth and desire to be active in the business community. Immigration attorneys often try to help their clients meet business owners, so check in with some of the larger firms to explore this option.

Strategic Buyer: Do some research with the help of a consultant. Know what type of companies in your industry strategic buyers acquire and which types of opportunities attract them. Are they looking for innovative products, entry into new markets, greater distribution, or star performers? You may have to focus on one or two of these areas and then streamline your company to become their perfect acquisition match.

---

[29] http://www.immigrationimpact.com, 2011/03/08/some-states-try-to-harness-the-economic-power-of-immigrant-entrepreneurs/

Look for companies consolidating smaller companies in your industry. They are searching for economies of scale, market expansion and specific product or customer assets.

Decide whether your company can deliver one or more of the key benefits that they don't already have that will earn greater market share and growing revenues. Select the top three targets and start steering your company toward goals and activities to make your operation even more attractive to those buyers.

Develop a game plan to build relationships with your target buyers. Attend the conferences they attend. Find out about their strategic goals by getting to know their top people. Search for ways to explore joint venture opportunities. Use public relations and social media to build your brand in the same way they do. That way, when you're ready to sell, they already know your company and, more important, they know you and your management team. When you're ready to sell, engage advisors to facilitate the introduction of the idea of acquisition to your selected buyers. *Do not attempt this discussion on your own*! Starting to talk about their making you an offer is one of the most common mistakes sellers make, often with disastrous results. Be pursued. Never show urgency.

Financial Buyers: Learn how PEGs acquire companies, know what's important to them[30] and learn how they manage the process of searching for the right acquisitions. A financial buyer is actually a group of investors who create a fund in which to invest in certain types of companies. Generally, their target acquisitions are good cash flow generators with high gross margins that can add value to the current slate of companies the fund owns. If your company has

---

[30] DiFranco, Jack. "The fine line between love and fear: Exploring the relationship between entrepreneurs and private equity" *Published in Timely Topics for Private Equity, Volume 4* The Association for Corporate Growth (ACG), Chicago, IL January 2011
http://www.acg.org/assets/1/news/ACG_GT_WP_Love&Fear.pdf

long-term contracts, subscription revenue, service agreements, and/or a business that generates more than 15% in profit margin reliably year after year, private equity may be the best option to be your exit partner.

As with strategic buyers, get to know which groups acquire in your industry. Many PEG firms look at more than 900 deals per year before selecting two-to-five deals to pursue. That means you may be courted, but never reach the offer stage. Use advisors to make introductions, *after* you prepare your company for sale. Look for PEGs and M&A advisors, such as investment bankers, through the Association for Corporate Growth (www.ACG.org).

Securing the amount you want means optimizing to reduce risk while increasing profitability. We outline the optimizing work in the next section, Section VI, Helm the Transition, and you will learn about optimization options to gain operational readiness to be saleable. But first, in order to understand how improving operational effectiveness can increase what a buyer is willing to offer in an acquisition, look at the Multiple Effect table below.

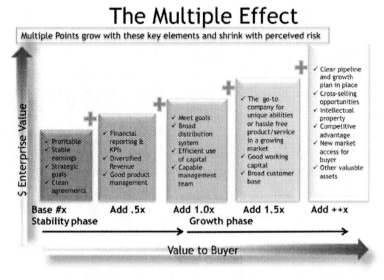

Fig. 8

Strategic vs. Financial Buyers

Each Multiple Attribute has a different weight depending on the type of buyer and the buyer's search criteria.

For example, for **Strategic Buyers**,[31] the reason they may offer a higher Multiple may be your company's ability to give them access to a product or market, as well as a distribution or sales network they can't build, or can't get timely access to themselves. Strategic buyers also like intellectual property, which extends their own product platform and customer base. Acquiring these assets often makes more sense than to spend the considerable time and resources necessary to build that capacity in-house. To attract this type of buyer, you may need to build or refine every attribute that builds Multiple points.

A **Financial Buyer**[32] or Private Equity Group cares mostly about the quality and volume of your cash flow, the effectiveness and depth of the management team, the capital structure, or the opportunity to reduce your company's costs by centralizing all non-core services into one of their platform companies. In this case, they hope the combined group of companies can complement each other strategically. PEGs want to see a growth plan that will differentiate your company from the competition and they want to see that your strategy is already under way and proving itself. Recognize that your company will probably be put up for sale within three-to-five years so funders can realize investment returns. The company has to be poised for more growth to be attractive to a new buyer.

What happens if your management team differs from either type of buyer? In some cases, a **Strategic Buyer** puts their own

---

[31] http://www.investtoexit.com/articles/strategic-buyers.html

[32] http://www.businessinsider.com/private-equity-and-strategic-buyers-a-distinction-without-a-difference-2011-5

management in place. A new acquisition may be absorbed into the strategic buyer's operation with your employees deployed to add value in new positions. Some strategic buyers let the acquisition continue to operate as a separate company and, therefore, a strong management team is very much key to getting a deal done. Your advanced research and preparation for the right acquirer will help you settle this question long before you get to the deal stage.

On the other hand, most **Financial Buyers** are not operators of companies, and that job stays in your company. While these buyers may have a lot to say about who is managing, they expect high performance and, if you've done a great job mentoring and positioning the right people in your firm to lead it, chances are the Financial Buyer will stick with the team in place. Realize these buyers will play an active role in your company, making suggestions, offering assistance, brokering deals and streamlining activities so that your operation maximizes returns. They know that making big changes post-acquisition can erode value quickly, so they work with a willing business owner judiciously.

Financial Buyers are also much quicker to use debt as a way to leverage growth. If managing with debt is not palatable to you and you intend to stay as part of the management team, a financial buyer might not be a good match. With a debt partner, comes a lot more scrutiny. Every Financial Buyer has its own preferences for structuring deals. Some look specifically at the 'financial engineering' opportunity, by assessing how much cash an acquisition can generate through leveraging assets by taking on debt. Other types prefer to use their operational experience to help their portfolio companies grow and acquire other related businesses to expand their 'platform' in an industry. You want a buyer whose intentions match your interests for the future of your company and your valuation goals.

Strategic Buyers will use their own cash, possibly stock, and they'll structure part of the transaction value as an earn-out to make the management team 'walk their talk' and prove their growth plan has legs. Smaller companies may use debt to acquire your company.

Both types of buyers and bankers want to see that your company has an obvious pipeline (good forecasting systems) for the near future, and that its selling to an industry that will likely continue to need what you have to offer for quite awhile. And, if no one else can deliver your product or service like you can, and you've proven it year after year, then chances are your company's name is already on their lips as the 'go to' company that buyers place first on their target list.

Knowing what is important to you regarding how the business operates and your involvement post-deal helps to attract the right buyer. There is no sense in working to attract a strategic buyer if you hate to reveal numbers to employees or potential competitors; and, be clear that one may be at your door with an offer faster than other types of buyers. Do the research first to find out which companies in your industry are consolidating through acquisitions, so you can make an informed choice and not be surprised later.

If you are exploring a **Management Buyout,** bankers and private equity groups need to see a great management team already in place (your chosen successor is a great leader and manager of people and resources, and there are other key managers with strategic and implementation skills) with a healthy pipeline and processes in place, too. More than any other succession option, the MBO requires the strongest cash flow to keep funding dividends and/or loan repayments. Your potential buyers are signing up to take on a lot of risk and debt to buy you out, so you want to know that your relationship is solid, with open communication, and that you have set up their foundation for success. For some types of businesses, a private equity group may be a good funding partner for your MBO, so you should explore options with a competent advisor.

The bottom line is that your firm has to have a future that looks bright without you in it, not just a shiny legacy of consistent earnings and a reputation that you have personally cultivated – *unless* you intend to work for the new owners post-acquisition. That's fine, but it's better to have that option and choose it, rather than to be forced into a management contract in order to get the deal done.

When Growth in Revenues Looks Doubtful

The relationship between the Multiple your buyer is willing to pay and your EBITDA directly correlates to the effort put in to grow the gross margin and bottom line, not necessarily sales or revenues. In this economy, when growth is limited, increase operational effectiveness *and* market attractiveness to reach your valuation goal. Working on both sides of the business decreases the risk for the future buyer because it will be obvious that your company will continue to produce reliable profitability. You become more adept at delivering what customers need – for less – and in a way that is more productive.

An Example

To illustrate what can reduce perceived risk, use Vince and Paul as an example. Their goal is to optimize their company so that it has an enterprise value of $8 million four years from now. Today, their company has an EBITDA over the last year of $2.5 million and they work hard in this economy to maintain $20 million of revenue in the construction industry.

Given these facts, is it possible that Vince and Paul's business will warrant an $8 million offer in four years? Let's look at it another way in Figure 6. Growth is difficult in new construction and projects often don't return the promising profit estimate after completion. To make their company attractive to the strategic buyer (a larger mechanical contractor), they must build their service business from 20% of revenues ($4 million) to 60% or

70% ($12 million to $14 million). Servicing HVAC in buildings that need regular maintenance is much more recession proof than new construction, so if they can do that, their gross margin should increase even if revenue isn't increasing. Because of the risk and depending on what happens to the construction industry, they may only be able to sell the service part of the business and have to wind down the construction side.

Over the next four years, Vince and Paul need to focus on growing the profit margin (EBITDA) from 7% to 10%, as well as moving their Multiple one full point to reach their goals. To improve operational effectiveness, they need to examine and improve how they track paperwork on projects (managed and billed). To improve project performance (which affects market attractiveness), they need to be better at managing labor variances. To get a better bottom line, they need key metrics to track performance on a weekly basis so they can spot and remedy problems that cause premature project losses. Service-based revenue has much better gross margins, so if fixed costs remain stable, they should be able to increase their profit margin by at least 3%. If Vince and Paul expand their service sales efforts with a growth plan, they can negotiate that additional point on the Multiple.

From UnSaleable to Saleable

Today	Millions	%	3 Years	Millions	%
Revenues	$20	100%	Revenues	$20	100%
EBITDA	$1.4	7%	EBITDA	$2	10%
Multiple	3X		Multiple	4X	
Today's Value	$4.2		Value in 3 Years	$8	
Valuation Goal	$8		Valuation Goal	$8	
Valuation Gap	$3.8		Valuation Gap	$0	

Fig. 9

By attending to these two internal goals (operational effectiveness and market attractiveness), Vince and Paul will transform their mechanical contracting company into the kind of acquisition that has appeal to Strategic buyers. All at a time when their competitors won't be able to understand how they achieved such performance! The bankers will be much more comfortable with their acquisition plans, so they will be more inclined to approve their maintaining a sizable operating line of credit and bonding ability that is so essential in the construction business.

How Investors View an Acquisition

Again, stand in the shoes of a potential buyer and take note of all the places in your company that might be a source of risk. Risk exists when you don't know for sure how, when or why your company is best able to deliver a return on investment. As the business owner, you've seen how your company makes money, loses money, breaks even or flourishes. You need to understand what drives each of these events. It's very difficult for anyone else to 'see in' and understand the ebb and flow of your company.

There is more to learn, but you should now have a cursory understanding of what your company might actually be worth, and why, as well as what type of investor you might attract. You may be ready to stand back and survey your optimization options, and develop a plan to increase your profit margin and multiple with a little more objective clarity.

Chapter 11 Summary

Learning how to view your company as investors will view it will help you understand how to attract a buyer and improve your company's performance.

To select the right kind of buyer, you need to be clear about your expectations for each of the hats for which you are responsible:

- Leave the company with the kind of legacy and payout you want
- Set the company up for future success
- Meet your own personal, financial and career/life goals

Section VI
Step Four: Helm the Transition

"Change is hard because people overestimate the value of what they have – and underestimate the value of what they may gain by giving that up."

James Belasco and Ralph Stayer[33]

What you will learn in this section:
- How to stabilize your company
- Demystify the activities that help optimize a company
- Where to focus the most time and attention
- How to lead change
- How to evaluate where to start making changes to stabilize profits
- Strategies to facilitate growth
- Refine where you are going
- How to get started on your exit path

---

[33] Belasco, James A. and Ralph C. Stayer, *Flight of the Buffalo: Soaring to Excellence, Learning to Let Employees Lead*, Grand Central Publishing, 1994

Chapter 12
Lead Your Company to that Certain Future

"Keep in mind that you cannot control your own future. Your destiny is not in your hands; it is in the hands of the irrational consumer and society. The changes in their needs, desires, and demands will tell you where you must go. All of this means that managers must themselves feel the pulse of change on a daily, continuous basis . . . they should have intense curiosity, observe events, analyze trends, seek the clues of change, and translate those clues into opportunities."

Michael J. Kami[34]

What you will learn in this chapter:

- Leading change
- Mindset adjustments to achieve stability
- See the company as an interdependent system
- Be responsible for your attitude
- Ask the right questions
- Set a new desired end result
- Build a Transition Plan

---

[34] Kami, Michael J., *Management Alert: Don't Reform – Transform! (Management Master, Vol. I)* Productivity Press 1994

There are very specific 'signs' investors seek that indicate that business owners have dealt with some of the risks of ownership. Initially, investors will focus on financial data and market opportunities as a first cut to see if the potential acquisition warrants further investigation (as shown in the Acquisition Evaluation Scorecard in Figure 5 on pages 112 – 114).

In order to prove whether cash actually flows and profits accumulate, buyers will look across all systems, reports, databases, customers, processes and agreements and history. They'll question management's focus to see what is actually happening. Wherever there is uncertainty, there is an element of risk. For every element of risk, a fraction of a point is lost in the Multiple and, therefore, a company's valuation decreases.

Then, they will want to get to know you and your management team, and a buyer will measure and compare what they hear and see in conversations with you. What you say and the attitude you display speak volumes to buyers who have combed through numerous potential acquisitions. They are looking for proactive managers who walk their talk, understand human behavior and clearly see the connection between people alignment and profitability. If you do your preparation, you will be demonstrating just what the buyer is seeking.

Readying a company for growth and sale isn't just about numbers – it's also about people. Preparation means you and your people must adjust, stretch and change in the two-to-four years before being ready for sale. Leading change, growth and succession often requires adjusting the leadership and management skills you developed as an operator. You may need to overhaul your own job description throughout this process. You will have to extract yourself from working in a functional role in the company and become the leader of this preparation process. *You will need to develop a transition plan.*

Your two-to-four years of preparation starts with five elements that must work in harmony for stability to take root:

- See the company as an interdependent system
- Be responsible for your attitude
- Ask the right questions about the purpose of what your company does and why you are doing it a particular way
- Set a new desired end result
- Build a Transition Plan

As we discussed in Chapter 3, many of the needed changes require a mindset adjustment. The next Exploration Exercise will help you see into your organization in an effort to recognize typical patterns that undermine stability. Reflect on whether your company falls into some of these traps. Then, review the answer key to see what you can do about it.

Exploration Exercise #5
Organizational Mindset Challenges

Clichéd thinking abounds today, and some of these belief systems and ways of working are detrimental to business health. Thoughtfully reflect on whether your company operates under these conventional wisdom mindsets and check all that apply. These mindsets are not wrong, they're just limiting to your company's potential to grow. You may want to complete this exercise yourself first, and then have a colleague evaluate you. Note the differences and assess whether you need to pay attention to making some changes. What do you believe? Check all that direct your thinking and action:

☐ Companies get work done best by dividing it into functional areas

☐ Revenue and EBITDA are the top key performance indicators

☐ If you watch the numbers carefully, the company will perform

☐ The buck stops at the top

☐ You have to persuade people to get their buy-in

☐ Management meetings are for making decisions

☐ The way to improve profitability is to cut expenses

☐ Margins are the responsibility of the CEO and CFO

☐ The best decisions are based on data

☐ The way to get more volume is to discount price

☐ You are in business to make money

☐ The best way to get things done is to take charge

Organizational Mindset Answer Key

- Companies get the best work done by dividing it into functional areas.

  The organization is best seen as a holistic system with work distributed across multiple departments; work collaboratively on developing solutions that meet customer and operational needs. It will increase productivity and reduce problems.

- Revenue and EBITDA are the top key performance indicators.

  Gross margin (revenue = cost of goods or services = gross margin) provides you with your best indicator for finding opportunities to improve profits. Increasing gross margin will increase profitability even if sales aren't growing.

- If you watch the numbers carefully, the company will perform.

  People who are aligned to strategic plans with well-defined, desired results, as well as specific responsibility for goals and working under clear authority and accountability, dramatically increase the company's performance.

- The buck stops at the top.

  The buck stops where responsibility, authority and accountability exist. Responsibility without authority renders employees powerless to act. Authority without responsibility is chaotic. Not knowing who is responsible, means you can't find the root of the problem. The buck starts with your setting and following a relevant organizational structure.

- You have to persuade people to get their buy-in.

  People buy into what they help create. If you are busy persuading, chances are you haven't collaborated with the people you are expecting to implement your concepts.

- Management meetings are for making decisions.

  Management meetings are for figuring out how to implement the decisions made. Then, meetings can be for reporting progress, maintaining alignment, planning, exploring impacts, innovation and change, and following up on current projects.

- The way to improve profitability is to cut expenses.

  The biggest gains to profitability will come from increasing prices in small increments and reducing costs to produce your product.

- Margins are the responsibility of the CEO and CFO.

  Help the managers who make decisions on your behalf everyday understand how these decisions increase or decrease gross margin.

  Invest in financial management education for your decision makers.

- The best decisions are based on data.

  If you only use data, you may be making the wrong decisions for the wrong reasons. Data helps inform a correctly framed problem, so start with the right question – what do our customers need and how can we best provide that in a way that ensures a return? But, the right decision is based on the collective practical wisdom, hunches, market information and experience, as well as data.

- The way to get more volume is to discount price.

  It is very difficult to make up the effects of a price discount with volume. It's better to help your sales people learn how to explore and offer other benefits to keep prices healthy, rather than sell the volume story.

- You are in business to make money.

  You are in business because you make or provide something a certain target market needs and values. In return, they are willing to pay you for that. If it doesn't meet their needs, they will switch to a company that does. Keep your functional hat on. Be a service and value provider and your reward is making money.

- The best way to get things done is to take charge.

  Only if you don't want to grow the company and want to do everything yourself because you don't want to take the time to train, mentor and discuss your expectations for performance and productivity. It's time to learn how to lead and delegate effectively.

See the Company as an Interdependent System

Observe your company as a system rather than a bunch of departments. Learn to see your organization from this holistic perspective, not a silo perspective. Every individual and every department has an interdependent role to play in the building and delivery of value to the customer, and you can't fix one area without attending to the others that depend on it.

Follow the trail of information as it is passes from one person to the next to find the problems. For instance, if you have a billing cycle problem, the trail starts with the time sheet or other labor and material input systems, and it winds its way through approvals, landing on several desks before it becomes part of the accounting system. It then turns into an invoice that arrives at your customer's place of business. The potential for problems lives in every hand-off, from person to person through each department, so you can't point at accounting and say they are to blame.

To begin this preparation work you need to engage your employees in an entirely new type of ongoing conversation. To find the trouble spots, generate ideas for innovation and gain buy-in for change, become a good listener, idea generator, explorer, decision maker, change agent and strategic planner.

Be Responsible for Your Attitude

Sometimes, it's tough being at the top – if what you do and say is different from the policies, values and guidelines you set for employees, your people follow by your example. If you let yourself off the hook, your employees will, too. If you blame, so will they. Leave behind a tendency to look for someone to blame when you discover a trouble spot and, instead, focus on finding the root of the process problem rather than the symptom of the problem, or the person who should have fixed it.

Blame in the atmosphere stifles information exchange and you won't be able to find the source of the problem. It's usually not the people at fault. Rather, it is missing processes or unclear roles, responsibility or authority problems that cause operations problems. If you acknowledge effort in working in the new proactive way, your employees will look for better ways to keep improving.

Ask the Right Questions

That's not to say that you shouldn't hold your managers and employees accountable and expect them to be responsible. However, more often than not, a single manager can't fix a systemic issue. It requires a cross-departmental team to hunt down the complex web of issues that contribute to order fulfillment not meeting customer expectations, or accounting not getting invoices out on time. A host of transactional activities that start outside these silos must take place before either department can achieve the desired managerial result.

To discover whether you have any of the telltale issues that stifle information exchange that often emanates from how the owner manages, look through the next Exploration Exercise to see into your organization in a new way. Then, review the answer key for help on how to shift your mindset to get out of the quagmire.

Exploration Exercise #6
Personal Habit Pattern Mindsets

The following is list of statements that describes thinking habits in which many of us are stuck. They are not right or wrong, but only ways of working that might not get us what we want. By choosing to recognize these habits, you can do something to address them.

- ☐ Getting it done fast (especially decisions) is satisfying.
- ☐ It's important to protect people from criticism.
- ☐ You often focus on what/who drives you nuts.
- ☐ When you want something done, you go to the person who can do it, not the person who should be responsible.
- ☐ If you need it done right, you do it yourself.
- ☐ The day starts with other people's agendas not yours – your email box.

☐ You often think along the lines of, "Another day, another crisis, what else can go wrong?"

☐ When two people come to you with a problem, you fix it and find a solution for them.

☐ When you have a concern with someone, you talk to the people around them, not to them directly.

☐ You often wonder if you are the only one who seems to care about . . .

☐ You like it when people do their work the way you would do the work.

☐ You have a lot of doubts.

☐ You share your doubts with others.

☐ When someone does something you don't like, you may make assumptions regarding their motive.

☐ You like to educate people about how to do things.

☐ It can be hard to put what you know into the discussion.

☐ You tend to forget what was agreed to in meetings.

☐ It can get confusing when trying to figure out what the company actually needs.

☐ You know you need to listen more, but you find it hard to focus on what others say.

☐ You find it easier to see how the other person is at fault.

☐ It can be hard to see how you may have contributed to the problem.

☐ You assume conflict will start if you bring up difficult issues, so you avoid pointing out what you notice.

☐ You tend to use words like 'always' or 'never' when raising issues with others.

☐ It is not easy for you to express appreciation or gratitude when others put in extra effort or go beyond the call of duty.

☐ It is not easy for you to acknowledge your own efforts.

Personal Mindsets Answer Key

- Getting it done fast (especially decisions) is satisfying.

  Yes, but did you solve the right problem? When considering time, quality and cost, you can only get two out of three results at any given time, and the third is sacrificed. Think about your desired result before you solve the problem.

- It's important to protect people from criticism.

  Feedback is not the same as criticism. Learn the difference and take the opportunity to mentor, laying out what might work better (show them how to think about it).

- You often focus on what/who drives you nuts.

  When you spend your creative and mental energy thinking about what you do want and not what drives you nuts, you'll get positive results.

- When you want something done, you go to the person who can do it, not the person who should be responsible.

  This is a red flag that indicates you don't follow your own organizational hierarchy, that you have unclear roles and responsibilities, that you have not transferred knowledge, and you don't hold people accountable. Without these structures, stability and, therefore, profitability is difficult.

- If you need it done right, you do it yourself.

  This mindset is good for sole proprietors and dangerous for businesses with employees. You send a message that you don't trust the people you selected to hire. If you are performing the task, you have the wrong person for the role, or you need to decide what you want to do with your time.

- The day starts with other people's agendas not yours: your email box and the crises of the day.

  Set aside ninety minutes each morning to work uninterrupted on your top priority projects that need uninterrupted thinking or collaboration time. Use the 'do not disturb sign'. Turn off email and focus. Let people work out their problems themselves. Grant clear authority.

- You often think along the lines of, "Another day, another crisis, what else can go wrong?"

  Your employees will emulate your thinking and actions. Is this how you want them using their minds? Chances are, if you and your teams focus on how to work with the problems, instead of reacting to them, they will be resolved. You are not a victim of circumstance unless you agree to be one.

- When two people come to you with a problem, you fix it and find a solution for them.

  The CEO's job is to set out the parameters and guiding philosophy under which the company operates. Help your people think through the problem, but let them come up with the solution and an action plan themselves. Your role is to revise and approve it, or else you're doing their jobs on top of your own.

- When you have a concern with someone, you talk to the people around them, not to them directly.

  By all means, collect feedback from others regarding a concern, but speak directly to the person involved first. It is the respectful thing to do. Make sure you have your listening skills turned up, and invite someone else in who has better listening skills than you if you know this is a problem.

- You often wonder if you are the only one who seems to care about . . .

If you care, say something. If you don't, then stop judging people about their degree of care. Things aren't completed for many other reasons, and it is not that they don't care. Use your curiosity to find out what happened rather than prove out your assumption.

- You like it when people do their work the way you would do the work.

When people don't work to their strengths[35] and attempt to imitate other people's way of working, the chances for success are fairly slim. Set useful parameters for when work is to be done or what is included in the solution, rather than how it gets done.

- You have a lot of doubts.

Doubts carry important information, so write them down. What are you trying to tell yourself? Extract the answer. Decide what you want to do about it. Collaborate on a solution with those responsible for that area once you know your desired result. Plan an action. Place in priority with other needs. Engage your team in the planning and implementation.

- You share your doubts with others.

See above. Don't share, unless you want help to come up with a solution; otherwise, you just sound critical or complaining. Doubt takes up a lot of time and mental energy.

- When someone does something you don't like, you may make assumptions as to their motive.

---

[35] One of the best investments you can make is to get to know your people's strengths. Get everyone to read and take the StrengthsFinder assessment by the Gallup Organization. Buy *Strengths Based Leadership* by Tom Rath and Barrie Conchie.

Ascribing motivation to someone is a sign that you think someone has power over you. Step back and see why your assumptions might have led you to that conclusion. Validate them. Ask yourself and the person you have doubt about (in a neutral voice) what they really meant. Chances are your sense of power and control will return when you have that reality-check.

- You like to educate people about how to do things.

  Make sure that people want and need what you have to offer before you launch into the lecture. Chances are, once people know your interests in sharing your knowledge, and they express their interest in learning, they may be more willing to hear it and use it.

- It can be hard to insert what you know into the discussion.

  When the discussion focuses on interpreting data, it can appear as if there is no room for other perspectives, such as a hunch about what to do next when the data doesn't clearly point to it. As the owner, make certain you set aside time in every meeting to collect qualitative input, too.

- You tend to forget what was agreed to in meetings.

  Use an agenda. Take notes. Plan out all decisions. Assign responsibility, set milestones and next steps. Delegate actions. Then, it's much more difficult to forget and change takes root.

- It can get confusing when trying to figure out what the company needs.

  Use a hierarchy of criteria or a decision tree to evaluate what the company needs. Check first to see what the market needs, what the customer needs, what new customers need to switch to your company, and then look internally at how your systems and operations need to change to meet the external needs. Your priorities will become much more apparent.

- You know you need to listen more, but you find it hard to focus on what others say.

  Listening is always a choice. You need to ask yourself why you choose to listen selectively. What you don't want to hear might be essential to moving forward.

- You find it easier to see how the other person is at fault.

  We are a nation of responsibility-avoiders, including the boss. It is humbling to discover that what you thought was a good action has negative consequences. But, it's how the owner treats the 'mistake' that can crush company productivity or unleash potential. Hold people accountable and look for the root cause in the process, rather than find fault in a person. Blame is a thief that will rob your company of productivity. Why invite the thief to the meeting?

- It can be hard to see how you may have contributed to a problem.

  The bad news is that many of the problems companies have are because of how the owner leads, communicates, acts and reacts. It might be easier if you ask yourself and your team how you are part of all the problems. It will be much faster to deal with them if you create an atmosphere of permission for your team to share such perceptions. To be ready to receive this feedback, you have to decide not to take it personally, not to defend your perspective and be willing to know when your people have hit the nail on the head. Then you are a powerful and effective leader people will want to follow and copy.

- You assume conflict will start if you bring up difficult issues, so you avoid pointing out what you notice.

  The apathetic statement, 'Whatever!' has created a world where it is just easier to put heads down and ignore the elephants in the room rather than be the bearer of bad news. See above for setting a permission-giving atmosphere.

- You tend to use words like 'always' or 'never' when bringing up issues with others

  The minute these words appear in a sentence (along with 'but', 'you', and colorful adjectives), people tend to hear blame and shut down. Brain capacity diminishes, and the opportunity to work through why something doesn't work well is lost. Use at your own peril.

- It's not easy for you to express appreciation or gratitude when others put in extra effort, or go beyond the call of duty.

  By investing in noticing effort, you engage employees in a new way that inspires their interest to perform the task better the next time. Saying a genuine "Thank you!" or noting something that particularly impresses you, or acknowledging difficulty of a task and a job well done will pay off in dividends – if you practice it consistently.

- It isn't easy for you to acknowledge your own efforts.

  It can be lonely at the top. No one stands around noticing all that you put into the job. Except you. Self-acknowledgement is essential for emotional and mental health. No one follows you around all day, so you are the expert on the subject. It sounds ridiculous, but people who regularly appreciate what they do for themselves, have far less stress, less resentment and more engaged employees.

Set a New Desired End Result

Once you are aware of the systemic issues throughout the company, you will want to refine your desired end result (DER), strategic goals and metrics so everyone is working together toward the exit date and valuation goal. Simultaneously, work with your managers to develop a transition plan to change and optimize operations. You set the DER, and managers develop the strategy and help employees implement action plans.

An investor wants to buy smooth-running companies where conversations result in a useful exchange of information and productive activity ensues. Communication should focus on improving alignment with your strategic goals, uncovering and remedying the blips in the system and acknowledging effective performance. These activities prove your company uses your capital effectively; when goals are set but not realized, uncertainty arises about management's ability to lead.

Removing communication barriers, such as the ones you identified in Exploration Exercises 4 and 5, following an optimal organizational structure and leading congruently are the prime contributors to productivity, performance and, therefore, profitability.

Additionally and beyond operational improvements, to optimize means to ensure that your product and service:

- Engages the right target market
- Solves the right problem in a hassle free way for this target market that creates customer loyalty and lifetime value for your company
- Is made and sold for a price that is in line or exceeds the gross margin of similar companies in your industry
- Delivers at the level of quality required to make your company stand out among competitors
- Has an evaluation feedback loop which helps your company continually innovate

Remember VPA, Vince and Paul's company? When research on potential acquirers showed that larger companies interested in consolidating small mechanical contractors were only buying those with a strong service component, VPA had to make a decision to invest further in that area of their business.

While they did have service contracts with most of the building owners, few contracts came from other sources – the service division didn't have a sales person. In an effort to win preferred maintenance contracts and not just bid work, they would have to learn how to consult with business owners so they will switch from one contractor to VPA. They would have to invest in marketing, brand building, customer service and better dispatching, as well as additional vehicles, tools and staff.

But, before they could do that, VPA had to uncover what elements might cause a building owner to become dissatisfied with its current supplier, and then come up with a plan to deliver a better package of services than their competitors. This key differentiating factor will prove to be the lynchpin in their growth strategy to win them new business, better gross margins and interest from buyers.

Your job for the next two-to-four years is to steer your company so your people become responsible enough for you to trust transferring knowledge and key relationships. Uh, oh. This means you might have to let go, get out of the way and trust others! Your new attitude toward communication and change may be the only sign that everyone needs to follow this path of change to get you the valuation you want. Don't be part of the problem – let your leadership and communication skills be the model for the solution.

Do two things and in this order:

- **Stabilize your company**: Lead in a way that uncovers the barriers so that they can be cleared out of the way to achieve your desired result, then

- **Grow the company**: Get out of the way, so managers show they can grow the company on their own.

Stabilizing the company is what PSWA had to do as outlined in their plan in Chapter 5. It means uncovering the root causes that contribute to poor profitability, inconsistent gross margins, poor sales growth, customer churn, employee attrition, and the daily frustrations that erode the company's ability to innovate. Stability also includes how and who manages, as well as who leads the functions of the company.

Having the right people in the right roles, with clear accountability and responsibility for a set of goals and key performance indicators, achieves stability. If the business has to rely on you to manage and lead for a specific function or set of functions, and you don't have other people who manage, the company is not stable.

Growth is possible when you have a firm foundation in place – a stable organization is comprised of people who have skills and the freedom to communicate effectively, and to deal with issues effectively and efficiently while also making the necessary changes to accommodate growth. Then, you also need to know that what you are producing or providing is needed, wanted and competitively packaged to attract and keep customers.

Build a Transition Plan

Your plan to close the gap and increase the Multiple your company is worth may require an independent perspective to help you see what works and what doesn't work with respect to internal stability, management capability, communication flow and growth opportunities. Internal stability is a direct result of management's ability to share and discuss information, perspectives and ideas without barriers. Therefore, most companies need to address their interpersonal communication (challenges) first, followed closely by getting the right managers or leaders on the bus. Then you can collectively begin work on setting goals and remedying those operational issues that create instability.

Close the Value Gap to Reach Your Exit Goals

To close the gap, you can spend a lot or a little time and resources, simply change fundamentals or really revitalize your organization. It's your choice. Just realize that the less you do, the wider the gap between what you want and what you will get – and recognize the lower the probability that your company will attract a buyer.

Pick your goals. If you want your company to be worth more than it is today and to be close to your industry's Multiple, then you will want to do a clear-eyed assessment of your company's strengths and weaknesses using the Acquisition Evaluation Scorecard on pages 130 - 132 as your guide. For each aspect that you rate lower, do the work involved to improve your company's attractiveness to investors. Select the stability actions in Chapter 13 and growth ideas in Chapter 14 to provide you with solutions for some of the typical challenges many companies face. These actions are what will improve your Multiple. Just as you need to select the type of investor you want to attract, you will need to show a top-notch operation to a buyer in order to be attractive as an acquisition, or to a lender to fund a buyout. Remember that improving your gross margin performance also increases your EBITDA, which also merits a higher valuation as long as it meets or exceeds your industry norms.

Chapter 12 Summary

Stabilizing your company is the first step toward gaining a higher Multiple and it must be done before growing the company. This means you will have to uncover the root of structural and interpersonal problems. You can remove typical obstacles when you examine how you lead, communicate and work. Employees will follow your lead, so be sure what you are signaling is the behavior attitude and approach you want your people to follow.

By identifying the actions you must take for stabilization and growth, you will identify the type of acquirer you want to pursue. This will require research, strategic goals and planning. Working to these goals should be your top priority, and your employees need to be aligned and working in tandem within these goals, so communicating the purpose of their work in the context of the goal is essential.

Chapter 13
Stability Actions

"Guarding knowledge is not a good way to understand. Understanding means to throw away your knowledge."

Thich Nhat Hanh[36]

What you will learn in this chapter:

- Suggestions and examples for increasing stability
- The flags that show you whether you should take a certain action in your organization

Taking any of these actions outlined in this book will increase the likelihood of your company being saleable because they all reduce risk. This work also makes your company more profitable so you, as the owner, are rewarded either way. Since you are an owner and primary investor, you have nothing to lose and everything to gain by doing this work.

We suggest that you hone your decisions to set a valuation goal, an exit date, a profit goal and a Multiple Goal. Each of these goals is a lever that contributes to the price a buyer might be willing to offer. In this section, we suggest a series of stability actions that will contribute to increasing your Multiple Goal.

---

[36] Thich Nhat Hanh October 11, 1926 is a Buddhist monk, teacher, author, poet and peace activist based in France.

Completing the Acquisition Evaluation Scorecard on your company, using the comparable guide for your industry and completing the exercises so far, you have a fairly good idea of the Multiple your company will earn at the moment. For instance, if you assess that your company is worth 4x EBITDA today, and the average Multiple paid to companies that get bought in your industry is 7x, you know that to be in the running, you will want to increase your Multiple by at least 2x if not 3x. The following actions in this chapter will help you narrow down which ones to select to get that Multiple growth. After you uncover your challenges as outlined in Chapters 3 and 13, these stability actions may make a huge difference in your operation.

As you review each suggested action, it may be helpful to ask employees or trusted individuals who know your company (suppliers, long-term customers) which of these you need to pay attention to, and there isn't a need to tell them you're thinking of selling. You want to improve your company, so it serves their needs better; and, this will be true no matter what your personal future holds. It can be difficult for an owner to recognize where pockets of instability exist in the company. This is especially difficult if your tendency is to think that individuals are at fault (rather than seeing that it is the processes or systems). More often, the problem of poor performance is that you haven't mapped out information exchange processes, such as who should provide what, by when.

Every company must serve the needs of a particular group of customers. This is how they make sales, but it is only part of the equation to make money. How you uncover and fill needs is what makes a company unique and saleable. The other part of the equation is keeping and using the money that you make to invest in growth, renewal and building your balance sheet.

Improving the Base Multiple

The first step to prepare your operation for sale is to improve the stability of your operation. To stabilize means to optimize your company. Optimize your company so that it serves customers, delivers value and retains a better percentage of the money it makes. There are four pillars of stability:

1. Financial
2. Operations
3. Customer Experience
4. Leadership

You may have more work to do in one or two of the pillars, but you need to look at all four to determine what needs attention, since they are all interdependent.

By taking these actions, you will increase the likelihood of attracting a buyer. Most important, for you as the primary investor, this work will increase your own return on investment.

You have built your company as a series of systems, processes, and knowledge that serves to deliver your products and services as promised. You have made innovations and improvement that keep old customers returning and new ones buying. You pay for all of that and, in return, you receive payment. The harder it is to for your managers and staff to transfer information through your internal systems, the more money it costs to deliver on customer expectations and less money stays in your company.

How to Find Typical Profitability Leaks

In our experience, regardless of the type of company, most businesses suffer from the same patterns that result in poor performance. As you read the descriptions, you may want a second opinion to see if your company is dealing with any of these issues.

Here are some examples of the root cause of company instability. Review the descriptions to see if your company suffers from these frustrations. Then make it a high priority to set up a project, a team and a mandate to develop remedies.

No Data or Poor Data: Your accounting and reporting system can't give you timely information. It is hard to uncover problem areas in your cost structure as they happen. Sometimes you have the data, but you don't have a report to make sense of it. For some companies, the reports you need are impossible with the software you currently use. For example, you want to have a report that provides timely indicators on labor variances in manufacturing, actual over budget, utilization rates, gross margin by customer or product, or contribution margin by customer or product.

Solution: Upgrade your accounting system and/or work with a financial management expert and accountant to build you the kind of reporting your business needs. Top priority. Then read the reports each week and attend to the exceptions.

Billing: Many companies struggle to send invoices in a timely manner due to missing information, unclear deadlines, interdepartmental communication conflicts and unnecessary complexity. Customers wonder about quality practices; your banker wonders about management's ability to manage cash flow.

Solution: Gather the representatives from all participating departments in a room and map out who does what and when. The gaps will reveal themselves and you will be able to build and agree to new processes.

Customer Service: Manufacturers are inconsistent with how much customer service to provide, so some employees over perform on some requests and others don't. There are no easy-to-follow lines of authority, manufacturer responsibilities and expectations of distributors. Unclear expectations breed mistrust.

Solution: Organize a multi-function customer experience team to track the complaints and set up new procedures, services and policies.

Customer Complaints: Your company has followed the same sales and service processes for years, and now it's 'just the way things are done around here' – so you are unaware of all the hassles customers encounter when dealing with your company.

Solution: You can resolve this problem by empowering a team of your employees with a mandate to rectify what doesn't work well for customers.

Pricing Problems: Pricing strategies are haphazard, rather than uniform, and changes are difficult to manage, which makes price increases or adjustments a complex administrative headache.

Solution: This is a multi-departmental problem. Improving the data tracking system so you can track each product is important – so is the latitude you give to sales people. Small pricing increases are great contributors to gross margin growth; you want to organize your pricing strategies so you can group them by product, by customer and by contribution margin. Then you can select small subsets to apply pricing increases, as well as test new price points and sales strategies.

When you resolve each of these problem areas, you can clean up profitability leaks. Are they easy or quick solutions? No. But the cost to your organization in delaying a remedy for any of them far outweighs the investment of time and focus. Depending on the number of employees you have and the number of issues you need to resolve, you can work on plugging these leaks simultaneously. Expect to spend six months to a year to see results.

Phase 1 of Stability

Profitability: Learn about how to find and stop the leaks in the income statement, and focus on working capital efficiency. Work to improve the gross margin and if you manufacture, distribute or retail products and services, examine how easy it will be to raise prices by one percent. Look for effortless ways to reduce product costs by one percent. If you provide services, analyze where actual labor costs chronically miss estimates. Upgrade the accounting system and/or your accountant, and use a controller or good accountant to get your accounting in order. Create useful expense categories so the accountant can perform a contribution margin analysis on each product or service. Use a financial management expert (not the controller) to help you analyze where the leaks are; schedule an audit.

Strategic goals: Decide what kind of reputation you want for your company. Develop a new desired result based on what you discover customers need so they don't switch to other providers. Transform these needs into your strategic plan, and analyze what needs to change in the company in order to deliver these needs; work with managers to make changes. Set metrics for revenue, fixed costs, contribution margin, accounts receivable and net profit. Set and approve budgets and forecasts; then manage according to that budget. Now performance reviews are possible to hold managers accountable to the vision and goals.

Stable Earnings: If you are resorting to using a growing line of credit to keep payroll afloat, look at your operation and check working capital efficiencies such as Accounts

Receivable and inventory days. Cut back and let go of those items that do not get performance results.

Focus on the Four Pillars of Stability

You must make improvements in all four pillars, not just in cost reductions to counterbalance these forces:

Financial: Regain pricing power to increase the value of a product for sale, reduce cost of goods sold to increase the margin left to pay expenses, set limits on billing cycles, work in progress and variances, and set and track budgets.

Operations: Optimize internal systems to serve strategic goals.

Customer Experience: Transform product and service offerings into solutions that resolve customers' perceived problems so that sales and loyalty can grow.

Leadership: Manage so that information flows, think through impacts, set goals, delegate, mentor, follow up, measure performance and follow the structure.

Stability is about optimizing the company so it delivers value and makes money. To build these four pillars of stability, you have to look at the company as a set of interdependent systems that contribute to the customer experience. Focus efforts on solutions that address the top six trouble spots that chip away at these pillars. Work to make improvements in all areas. Remember that the Multiple increases as you improve and refine each of these areas:

- **Become informed** about how the company actually makes and retains money, and discuss your findings with managers and decision makers. Keeping people in the dark makes profitability difficult, and if the owner can't explain how and why the company makes or loses money, managers won't know either.

- **Listen to Customer Perspective to Improve Pricing Power & Quality** - Misunderstanding your customer's needs or your target market results in perceived poor quality, incomplete product or service solutions and missed opportunities. Maintain pricing power by being the best from your customer's perspective rather than company assumptions.

- **Focused & Respected Organizational Structure Generates Responsibility** - Unclear roles, responsibilities, accountability and expectations should match strategic vision and goals. Track and remedy issues through key performance indicators, and use and respect roles rather than appease personalities.

- **Predictable Standards of Practice Produce Expected Outcomes** - Unclear performance expectations of staff and managers, misalignment of strategic goals and work performed means the company is led by reactions rather than pro-action.

- **Information Exchange Drives Quality** - Inconsistent deadlines for information hand-off increase reliance on credit lines. Missing detail, inaccuracies, and poor hand-off practices block paper flow, invoicing and collections. Set procedures, standards and dates for every document that transfers hands.

- **Removing Communication Blocks Powers Motivation-** A culture of blame blocks communication internally among departments and it is highly correlated to apathy. Critical information hides by competitive game playing, and inaccurate and negative communication is like having leaking oil in an engine. The leader sets the tone through action, body language, tone of voice and focus.

For more information on how to do this work, you may want to view the webinars and online learning videos and implementation guides at www.endeavorIQ.com.

Finding Profitability Leaks

In the technical consulting firm, PSWA, discussed in Chapter 13, Peter and his partners had to learn about and trace their trouble spots to become saleable and improve profitability. They started with the biggest concern – the company can't consistently deliver their projects on time and on budget. You will discover that the root of the problem causes a ripple effect that dominos through the company. They learned that this problem causes the following cash flow leaks:

- It forces them to compete on price rather than ability, which makes it harder to compete to get work, as well as blocks rate increases. Less revenue places more pressure on the credit line.

- Charge-out rates stay low which keeps gross margins low.

- Reliance on a growing line of credit because they can't calculate work in progress, which affects their ability to invoice monthly.

- Poor hiring and firing decisions because they can't track who is performing and who isn't. Therefore, they have missing capability gaps and poor quality work; however, they don't have a way to address these concerns with their people since difficult conversations in performance reviews don't happen. Everyone is told their work is 'excellent' regardless of what really happens.

For PSWA, the first steps to rebuilding the pillars of stability are to become informed by bringing in a new managerial accountant who is able to make sense of the numbers, educate the owners and help build some financial metrics. This effort will also require a new financial system that can give them the reporting they need. The partners make a commitment to learn how to read the financial reports and extract information critical to decision making.

They retain a consultant to help them set a new vision that includes becoming the 'go-to' company for a very specific set of service offerings for which they know their market pays a premium. Their strategic goals include financial, as well as aspirational metrics, such as expanding the number of high margin clients needing specialized services. They ask managers to participate in strategic goals, and then they ask managers to participate in developing plans for the changes needed to achieve the goals. They select project quality as a priority and work with a cross-functional team to write a set of definitions for the entire company; what quality looks like in action on projects, in the culture, and through communication. Concurrently, they engage clients in in-depth conversations about what it is like to work with PSWA and what they could do to improve performance and client relationships.

Phase 2 of Stability to be Prepared for Growth

Once you track profitability leaks and improved stability, you have improved your Multiple by at least 1 point. If you want to increase the leverage power of your Multiple, continue reading. You and your team are now able to take on growth actions, and you and your team are ready for the next optimization opportunities that will set the stage for your growth.

How to Increase Another Point in the Multiple

Good Product Management: Track who buys what and why. Focus on the improving relationships with buyers of higher contribution margin products or services. Ensure the product or service has the level of quality that customers demand. Does the supply chain deliver the quality of raw material needed? Are there services and benefits that you can build into the product so that it is a solution, not just a widget? Adding services to products so there is less hassle or work for the customer is an example of a solution. Restaurants add valet parking. Manufacturers have a shelf-stocking program for retailers. Grocery stores offer gluten-free product sections. Distributors offer delivery and installation. Technology firms make software 'point and click' to increase adoption.

Set up financial reporting and KPIs: Measuring any activity is the fastest way to find what needs improving – pay attention to it! You can read more about key performance indicators at the Advanced Performance Institute.[37] For example, if you are making things, track labor and material variances. Discover where there are variances and what causes them, and then help people learn how to make the behavioral and system changes that reduce the variance. If you are selling services, then you are selling your people's knowledge, productivity and relationship-building skills. Set up a standard by department and then ensure utilization rates get to 75% or 80% for billable staff. For accounting, measure the time it takes to send invoices and bring in accounts receivable.

Your banker should have some helpful guidelines and ideas to improve cash management. Your accountant can help you streamline your paper flow to meet the new deadlines you set for getting invoices out in time to reduce reliance on your credit line. In manufacturing, you want to

---

[37] Advanced Performance Institute API http://www.ap-institute.com/Key%20Performance%20Indicators.html

track gross margin by product from the bill of material, as well as safety, waste, inventory turns and types of products sold over different parts of the year. You will also want qualitative KPIs that measure employee well being and engagement. The Gallup Organization[38] pioneered and developed twelve questions that measure engagement[39] and it discovered that month-to-month consistency is critical, as is the ability to keep asking for and incorporating customer feedback.

Diversified Revenue: Decide that no one client or customer provides more than 20% of gross revenue annually. Develop a strategy to invest resources in acquiring new clients. Put your people with the best relationship-building skills on the project. Learn how to say, "No," so you can afford to say, "Yes" to the best opportunities that meet all of your goals.

The TIME FRAME TO IMPLEMENT these types of change is twelve to fifteen months.

When PSWA finally got their accounting system reorganized, they analyzed the contribution margin to see which clients were most profitable, as well as which services in which to invest for business development. This analysis helped them to discover that the largest client, the one who consumed the most time, resources and talent, actually paid them the least amount of money. In one month alone, 40% of their revenue came from that single client.

If you are in a similar situation, you can't afford to keep saying 'yes' to that client because the risk is too high. What would

---

[38] The Gallup Organization http://www.gallup.com/consulting/52/employee-engagement.aspx

[39] Workforce, Gallup's 12 Employee Engagement Questions http://www.workforce.com/section/hr-management/article/12-questions-measure-employee-engagement.html

happen if that client switched to another provider of services or product next month? Diversifying so no one client makes up more than 20% of all revenue is an important goal to set. Yes, it may take a few years to shift focus and to continue to service that dominant client strategically. Make sure you service new clients with your talented star performers, too, so new clients stick with you. Set up a strategic initiative to plan how to do this. A great starting place is to assign responsibility to someone for nurturing new clients. This person should have equal authority to current client account managers.

Phase 3 of Stability to Ignite Growth

If you want to close the gap to your exit goals even further and increase the probability of finding a buyer, go to the next level and work on these issues to gain an even higher Multiple.

How to Upgrade 2 Points in the Multiple

Meet your strategic goals: Show that your management team can set goals, budgets and forecasts, and then manage the company to reach these goals. Keep the paper trail according to what you plan, how you accomplish the plan and set up a dashboard so all employees can see how the company is doing – and, what *they* are doing to contribute to your success. You should set the strategy, but your managers should be responsible for planning how to implement and meet their own deadlines.

Business-to-Business Ideas – Broad High Performing Distribution System: Track distributor performance by contribution margin. Let go of the non-performing distributors and set better goals and clear expectations for the higher performance distributors. You might need to develop better reporting metrics and mentor under-performing channel partners so they can meet these metrics. Explore with them and implement what can be done so they can function in top form for their customers.

Business to Consumer: Revitalize the experience of buying from your place of business. Stand in the shoes of your customers and brainstorm what would make people want to come back repeatedly. It is the atmosphere, the way your people interact with your customers that draws people to return?

Efficient Use of Capital: Invest in your goals. Do the research and examine impacts of investments before you make decisions. Put capital where it will amplify contribution margins and minimize costs. Don't let the credit line creep up if you don't know exactly why it's rising. Set goals to pay it down and work on increasing the gross margin.

Capable Management Team: Set performance expectations for staff and mentor them to help achieve these goals. You set the strategy, provide performance reviews and foster two-way conversations for feedback. Encourage staff to be creative and empower them in reaching these goals – this means trusting them to achieve results by setting milestones. Getting their buy-in is essential, because people follow what they help to develop. For success, be supportive, fair, firm, appreciative, real and responsible in your leadership. Hold yourself and your team accountable through leading by example.

TIME FRAME TO IMPLEMENT? 12 – 18 MONTHS!

Don't be like PSWA who spent too much time and energy in fighting with each other over the effects of unintended consequences of their decisions. When managing to goals, a high performance team explores the consequences and implications *before* deciding on the action plan that includes reviewing and changing their own roles. If the PSWA partners don't have the skills or interest in learning, they should consider hiring a full time general manager or CEO. Will you take a cut in pay to afford to bring in the leadership talent to become saleable? Short-term pain can lead to long-term gain.

Chapter 13 Summary

Most organizations have profitability leaks and are missing critical stability pillars. It is a normal part of the entrepreneurial maturity map. Companies go through numerous growth phases and outgrow their internal systems, indicators, and communication strategies. Without knowing where to look, employees and owners develop coping strategies rather than proactive management.

The typical patterns that prevent stability are tied to the financial performance 'above the gross margin' line. Making changes here will generate far greater results than working below the expense line.

Chapter 14
Growth Actions

"Many of life's failures are people who did not realize how close they were to success when they gave up."

Thomas A. Edison[40]

If you have implemented some of our stabilization actions, you will notice within six to eight weeks that your bottom line should be improving. Now that you're working on stabilizing, it's time to add the core strategies that will make your company the ideal acquisition target. If you want your management team to buy you out over time, the financing source (bank, private equity group) will have some advice about where to focus. Bring them in early to know how to shape your company to qualify for financing a buy-out. Do the research, make the decision and steer the company so it is most attractive to your company's ideal buyer.

How to Upgrade 3 Points in the Multiple

Be the Go-To Company: If you have stabilized your company, you are now ready to amplify your brand and

---

[40] Thomas Alva Edison 11 February 1847 – 18 October 1931 was an American inventor, scientist and businessman who developed the phonograph, motion picture camera and the light bulb.

celebrate core competency, as well as zero in on a market and a need that your firm answers better than any other competitor. You want to become the first company that comes to mind for your target market – the company that your customer can rely on to get it right, provide a great customer experience and provide unique and predictable services that complement your products other companies lack.

Look for the Opportunities: If you look at your company from the outside in, does it appear that you are giving customers the best experience? Where can you offer service or add value for which customers may be willing to pay? Look at the entire Customer Experience and collect the complaints. Yes, the complaints! In every complaint is an opportunity to solve a problem. Turn products into end-to-end solutions, and partner with other companies to achieve complete service. People buy solutions to their issues, rather than what you have to sell. Listen to the good and the bad news by asking questions in an effort to gain deeper understanding. The reward is customer loyalty and added revenue, and both are vital elements of removing risk of future sales for a buyer.

Good Working Capital: If you deploy capital in support of goals and you are reaching them, banks will see there is cash flow able to support an injection of growth capital. To become the go-to company, open a new market and invest in innovation if the market supports it – or, hire a star performer with a big network in your target area. Don't be afraid to shut down poorly performing products, markets or distributors and redeploy assets before the writing is on the wall.

Do the Right Things Correctly: You built your company by investing in critical relationships with prospects, customers, influencers, suppliers and advisors. These relationships are also the lifeblood of your company's future. Keep these connections strong; ask customers and distributors what the company can do to make their lives easier and improve their futures. Give back and you will always receive more. Strong ties make it easier to introduce the next owner and your management team without the fear that relationships will fall apart when you leave.

Broad Customer Base: If the economy is coming back strongly outside your geographic scope, explore how can you can access and service that market or industry. When you are the go-to company and you've done the brand building to get that recognition in a market, it's much easier to enter new geographic or industrial markets and diversify revenue, as well as reduce exposure to a single economic cycle.

TIME FRAME TO IMPLEMENT? 2 – 4 YEARS!

How to Upgrade 4 or more Points in the Multiple

Add the Secret Sauce

To be truly saleable, most companies must have a growth strategy in order to be attractive for sale. If your company is in a highly competitive industry, such as technical consulting, where one firm is a good substitute for another, your company needs a secret sauce solution that solves a big problem in a robust way for the target market.

Secret sauce gives back the control of your pricing to you, as well as providing market power. The secret to the sauce is usually a set of intangible attributes that are hard to copy. For example, sample ingredients include your response time, a 'can-do' attitude and the depth of experience of your team that can point to the root cause of problems. Intangible attributes also include the way your managers handle problems or conflict, the transparency of how you conduct business, the rigor of your methodology, how you help your clients through change, the way you treat people, the well-thought out end-to-end product and service solution, as well as the inspiration you provide when helping customers. In Business to Consumer markets, it's the fun, the free information, the care and the uniqueness of your offering that makes people pick your business to garner their loyalty.

Whew!

Last Step – The Succession Plan

Now that you have stabilized and instituted a growth strategy to close your valuation gap, you need to think about succession plans for you and those shareholders who will be leaving. Map out the roles that you need to replace, and think about the skill sets that the company will need, not just your skill sets. Create a job description and then determine what salaries you will pay for this type of role. Prepare a financial analysis to determine if the company can afford to bring on this person (people) and the date it will be feasible. You may have to step aside and reduce your salary to achieve this transition.

The goal is to find the right person and then let them demonstrate they can lead the company, as well as achieve expected targets for at least four quarters of earnings before you are ready to put your business on the market. Plan to spend the first three months training them in all aspects of the business. A good way to do that is to have them work a day or two in each role they will manage. Then introduce them to key clients and suppliers so they start to build relationships. Go with them to see clients for a while to demonstrate your trust and commitment, and show your clients you aren't disappearing from the scene.

The second quarter, you or all partners or shareholders who will be leaving the company, should start to take off several days per month to allow their successors and the rest of the company to get used to the new leadership arrangement. The third quarter, if all is going smoothly, leave for an extended period. Spend the fourth quarter allowing the new team the freedom to operate the company with regular check-ins from you.

The company is now ready for sale. Start to contact and interview Mergers and Acquisitions advisors to begin work attracting the ideal buyer for your company. Even if you are planning to sell to managers or family, use an M&A advisor to represent your interests; package your offering so it can find the best financial partner to handle the negotiations. Don't compromise your company's future by not using an intermediary. Rick and Jenna are still paying the price today, four years after they attempted to sell their business to their COO. Pay the commission – it's worth every penny!

Chapter 14 Summary

When a company is not wrestling with the problems inherent at the instability stage, innovation, creativity and opportunity bubble up from employees and customers alike. The company is now prepared to take on bolder projects and it has cash flow and profits to invest in the future; it can effectively realize a return on these investments.

The biggest growth opportunities come from getting closer to the concerns of the marketplace. The owner or management team needs to be spending time at the forefront of the industry, expanding networks, finding joint venture partners, and connecting with customers to find gaps in offerings that can be valued.

Coming up with growth opportunities is only half of the equation. The work of leading growth should belong to the successor management team. Help set them up for success by working with them and slowly withdrawing your input while you're monitoring results.

Always invest in advisors for all stages of this process. You have one shot at making your company saleable and finding the right buyer. If you haven't done it before, don't try to become an expert. Selling a business is complicated, frustrating and full of unexpected potholes.

Chapter 15
How to Get Started

"There's a difference between interest and commitment. When you're interested in doing something, you do it only when circumstances permit. When you're committed to something, you accept no excuses, only results."

Art Turock[41]

What you will learn in this chapter:

- What motivates you
- How to take the first step
- How to stay committed

You may be confused or daunted by all of this information and you may be uncertain about what to do first. The first decision is to decide you want to do this work to discover what your company is worth, and that you want to close the valuation gap by doing the work to achieve a sale. If all shareholders agree, then the job is to stay intentional to find the answers that will work for you, your partners and your particular situation.

---

[41] Turock, Art *Invent Business Opportunities No One Else Can Imagine* Diane Publishing Co 2002 http://www.turock.com/

Once you handle reality, you know what your company might be worth. Maybe you discovered your gap is not as big as you had thought. Perhaps you know who your potential buyer is. No matter what your new awareness, the next step is to commit to a course of action. Hone your Goals and Decisions by learning, asking for help, getting resources in place and making concrete plans for action.

Regardless of your game plan, this work involves changing how you think, act and communicate. You may be changing how the company is structured, how it does business and how it operates on a day-to-day basis. Leading change can be a challenge if it is not your natural inclination, and self-awareness transparency in your communication and strategic planning skills are critical.

If you now know how to make these changes, but you aren't sure if you have the skills to change the business, then retain the services of a good business coach. That coach should read this book – they must be able to confirm they know how to help you achieve the Multiple goals selected to prepare your company for sale. If you can afford your replacement sooner, have them read this book to see if they understand what you need. Work with the new recruit to create a strategic plan to achieve these Multiple goals.

But, before you do anything, you first have to determine your own personal intentions. Write them down and look at them often to keep yourself on track, then:

- Complete all the exercises in the book.

- After that, pull out the elements from the exercises that need to be part of your action blueprint for each step of the framework.

- Make another list of items that you will want to educate yourself about regarding becoming saleable. Will you seek targeted online advice from various sources, such as

MakeYourBusinessSaleable.com, which provides monthly video training? Will you talk to your accountant? Make a list of the resources and people you need to connect with and perform the research you want to do.

- Then follow the instructions to do a financial and personal reality check. With this exploration, you will reveal what is and what is not important to you.

- Now that you have an understanding of what you really want and what your company needs to do to prepare to be profitable and saleable, you have some choices to make.

- Get any personal or professional guidance to help you make these choices and develop plans. Make a list of people in your network that would help you find the right advisors:

_____

_____

- Schedule time as soon as possible to contact your network so you quickly get the advice you need. Two-to-four years can fly by before you know it, so begin now so you will be ready.

The greatest gift you will ever give yourself is that of your own time and energy. When you put what is important to you on your schedule, and keep the appointment like you would with any other person, your world changes. Your productivity soars along with your pride, and when you are accomplishing things, life looks more promising because you feel a sense of momentum. When you sense momentum, you are happier. When you are happier, so are the people around you.

Waiting, however, can undo all of your hard work. For some people, the pain of staying the same is safer and more comfortable than the contemplation of the pain of changing.

So take a moment to pause right here and decide to choose your life path. What do you really want?

Here is what is possible when you prepare and implement the saleability blueprint to transition the ownership of your business:

- Employees take on more responsibility for management, sales, operations and organizational development leaving you free to lead strategy.

- The issues that plagued your profitability for years become stories to reminisce over with the managers who helped you fix the leaks.

- The base of customers that you have grows and their loyalty to your brand expands.

- The headaches that used to keep you up at night transform into ideas that make you leap out of bed in the morning.

- Opportunities that you had to say 'no' to in the past are now well within your grasp.

- People who wouldn't consider doing business with your company are now forging new partnerships with you.

- Star performers who would never have selected your firm as a place to rise up in their careers are now jockeying for the top spots in your company.

- Strategic buyers call you to see if you might be interested in selling the company.

- Return on your investment actually moves higher into double-digit territory, maybe for the first time.

- You look forward to letting go of the business because you are moving to a more vital, purposeful future, secure in the knowledge that your company will thrive under new ownership.

- You are paid the value you had always hoped for, and that you never dared to think was possible for all the years you have invested in making the company what it is today – a profitable, great place to work that delivers value for its customers and shiny returns for its owners.

If you have made the decision that you want these outcomes, then your next step is to complete this final Exploration Exercise so that you have a game plan to follow.

If you have not made the decision to take charge of your company's future, regardless of which exit method you choose, set a date in your calendar for when you will make that choice.

If that date goes by and you haven't decided, recognize that you have made a choice, regardless. You choose status quo. That's fine, as long as your recognize that for yourself.

Exploration Exercise #7
Your Blueprint Game Plan

PERSONAL HAT

1. When I sell my company, I want to take away $ _____ .

2. My best guess is that my company is probably worth $ _____ today.

3. The difference between what the business might be worth (answer 2) and what I want to take away from selling the company (answer 1) is $ _____. This number is called the Opportunity 'Gap'.

4. I would like to sell in year _____, which is _____ months/years from now.

5. If there is a gap in value as discovered in answer 3, will I do what is necessary to prepare the company so it is worth more to a particular type of buyer?

    Yes _____ No _____

6. By preparing the company so it is saleable, I will be able to do the following things for myself and my family:

    _____

    _____

7. Post sale, I want to be able to:

☐ Keep working in my company for the new owners to build it to the next level in the role of

_____

☐ Transition in a new leader and leave after _____ years

☐ Consult to the new owners

☐ Sit on the board

☐ Have no role in the company

☐ After I have sold my company, my next step in life is to

_____

_____

☐ The hardest part for me regarding selling my company will be

_____

_____

☐ If I can't sell my company, my backup plan is to (check all that apply):

    ☐ Continue as is

    ☐ Hire a manager to work under me

    ☐ Hire a president to run the company for me

    ☐ Sell to employees

    ☐ Find a partner and sell it to them over time

    ☐ Wind it down

    ☐ Keep going until it is saleable

    ☐ Learn about how to make it saleable

    ☐ Grow it until it is saleable

    ☐ Other (specify)

_____

_____

8. My top preference(s) is to:

    _____

    _____

9. If I can't sell my company for the amount that I really
   want, my backup plan for my retirement financial needs is
   to (check all that apply):

   ☐ Sell it for the offer amount, even if it is lower than my
      desired number

   ☐ Reduce my financial requirements/lifestyle

   ☐ Consult back to the new owners of the company for
      additional income

   ☐ Get a job

   ☐ Invest it all and live off the interest, if possible

   ☐ Start another company

   ☐ Live in a country that has a lower cost of living

   ☐ Other (specify)

      _____

      _____

10. My top preference(s) is to:

    _____

    _____

SHAREHOLDER HAT

11. If I (and, my shareholders) want to close the gap between
    what it is worth today and what I want to sell it for, it may
    take me two-to-four years to do this preparation, and it
    will require consulting with advisors to make changes.
    Am I willing to make that investment, time and effort?

    Yes _____ **No** _____ If the answer is no, go to question
    19.

12. I now know that I need to address the following issues in order to be able to sell my company. Read the list and put them in order based on what needs attention first.

_____ Profitability

_____ Management team

_____ Roles, accountability, authority & responsibility structure

_____ Goal setting and metrics

_____ Marketability of products/services

_____ Communications

_____ Internal systems and processes

_____ Organizational alignment

_____ Growth strategy

_____ Other (specify)

_____

_____

13. Do we have the right people in the right roles to make these changes so that the work of making the company saleable will occur? Mark Yes, Not sure or No for each.

Company Leadership	(Yes	Not Sure	No)
Department Leadership	(Yes	Not Sure	No)
Operations	(Yes	Not Sure	No)
Marketing/Sales	(Yes	Not Sure	No)
Finance	(Yes	Not Sure	No)
IT	(Yes	Not Sure	No)
HR	(Yes	Not Sure	No)
Manufacturing	(Yes	Not Sure	No)
Other (specify)			

_____

_____

FUNCTIONAL HAT

14. By preparing the company so it continues after I leave, I will be able to provide the following benefits for my:

Company

_____

_____

Employees

_____

_____

Customers

_____

_____

Suppliers

_____

_____

Family

_____

_____

Community

_____

_____

15. Knowing myself, my partners and my team, the challenges (refer to Chapter 3) that might make doing this preparation work difficult are:

Organizational (Structural Challenges)

_____

_____

Interpersonal Barriers

_____

_____

Personal Thinking Habits

_____

_____

Other

_____

_____

16. Reviewing your answers in the previous question, which areas of your company have these challenges? Check all that apply by marking 'S' for Structural Challenges, 'B' for Interpersonal Barriers, and 'P' for Personal Thinking Habits. Then count the type and number of challenges in each area:

☐ Financial

☐ Product

☐ Service

☐ Supplier

☐ Customer

☐ Operations

☐ Systems

☐ Emotional and thinking habits

☐ People interaction

☐ Marketing

☐ Sales

☐ Existing agreements

17. Referring to the previous question, which areas(s) of the operation have the most challenges? Check the top three that apply:

☐ Financial

☐ Product

☐ Service

- ☐ Supplier
- ☐ Customer
- ☐ Operations
- ☐ Systems
- ☐ Emotional and thinking habits
- ☐ People interaction
- ☐ Marketing
- ☐ Sales
- ☐ Existing agreements

18. I have the following reactions when I look at these challenges. Write down your thoughts, feelings, frustrations, questions, concerns or doubts about each challenge area. When you meet with your Exit Planner, share the results of these exercises and especially these reflections. It will help you start remedying them much sooner.

_____

_____

19. Based on your reflections, which areas do you think you can remedy yourself with the help of your team?

- ☐ Financial
- ☐ Product
- ☐ Service
- ☐ Supplier
- ☐ Customer
- ☐ Operations
- ☐ Systems
- ☐ Emotional and thinking habits
- ☐ People interaction
- ☐ Marketing

☐ Sales

☐ Existing agreements

20. Based on your reflections, in which areas do you think you will want help, another perspective or advice

☐ Financial

☐ Product

☐ Service

☐ Supplier

☐ Customer

☐ Operations

☐ Systems

☐ Emotional and thinking habits

☐ People interaction

☐ Marketing

☐ Sales

☐ Existing agreements

21. Which of the following Stability Solutions will you want to institute?

- Financial Pillar
  - o Finding profitability leaks
    - ▪ Accounting System
    - ▪ Billing Process
    - ▪ Customer Service
    - ▪ Customer Complaints
    - ▪ Pricing
  - o Working capital efficiency
  - o Diversify revenue sources
- Operations Pillar
  - o Organizational structure

- o Information exchange
- o Set strategic goals
- o Implement strategic plan
- o Set up key performance indicators
- Customer Experience Pillar
  - o Listen to customers' perspectives
  - o Organize a team that will reinvent customer experience
  - o Track contribution margin by client & product
  - o Broaden distribution channel
- Leadership Pillar
  - o Be the example
  - o Predictable standards
  - o Performance goals
  - o Removing communication blocks
  - o Empower management team
  - o Find management team

22. Which of the following growth strategies will you start to research?

- Be the go-to company
- Add services and other customer-valued benefits to products
- Track progress on all goals in which you are invested
- Deepen and extend company relationships
- Explore potential new markets and new industries geographically
- Innovate by adding a 'secret sauce'

23. Who will lead your company through the transition from now until the time you sell? Check all that apply.

☐ I will lead the company until the sale closes

☐ I will lead the company until I can find a new General Manager

☐ I will lead the company until I promote the right person to be second in command

☐ I will turn over the daily leadership to my current second in command, and work full time on building and implementing our saleability plan

☐ I will share leadership with my partners until we find the right next leader in the year before we want to sell

☐ I will train and mentor a committed family member to take over my functional roles

☐ I will train and mentor a committed family member to take over as CEO

☐ OTHER (specify)

_____

_____

_____

_____

☐ The date for this transition plan to start is

_____

Above all, remember why you need to make these preparations:

- **Make Your Choices Now, so Circumstances Don't Make Decisions for You.** What would happen to the value of your company if you suddenly had to find a buyer due to disease, divorce or even your own or a key employee's death and you couldn't sell it? Would it be in saleable condition?

- **Change your Family's Fortunes.** What would happen to your ability to retire and your family's future if you couldn't sell your company?

- **Do your Part for Economic Renewal.** What will happen to your employees, your town or community and your customers if you had to close the doors rather than sell your company?

- **Remember the law of supply and demand**. For buyers, there are many more companies on the market from which to select. What you are about to do is to make your firm more compelling and attractive to specific buyers in comparison to other companies in your industry space.

- **You are an Investor.** In the process of doing this work, not only is your return on investment going to increase, so will the return for your community, customers and employees. And, as a result, you will have done your part for economic rejuvenation in this country, and everyone benefits from this effort.

Whatever route you take, start the process now. You will find a lot of support out there if you look for it. Now you know what you really want, and you're armed with the information you need to talk to your banker, the SBA, the Chamber of Commerce and other advisors to find a competent team to help you. Read books.

Watch webinars on these topics at www.spiritwest.com. See the Appendix for a list of resources.

Chapter 15 Summary

Now you know all four steps regarding how to make your business saleable. You have identified all the areas in which you will want to improve in order to qualify for financing or to be attractive to your ideal acquirer. Your blueprint is ready. Now, all it needs is for you to push the ignition switch. Is it going to be worth your while?

Let's find out in the next chapter . . .

Chapter 16
Is it Really Worth it?

"Until one is committed, there is hesitancy, the chance to draw back, always ineffectiveness. Concerning all acts of initiative (and creation), there is one elementary truth the ignorance of which kills countless ideas and splendid plans: that the moment one definitely commits oneself, then providence moves, too. A whole stream of events issues from the decision, raising in one's favor all manner of unforeseen incidents, meetings and material assistance, which no person could have dreamt would have come his or her way."

William H. Murray[42]

What you will learn in this chapter:

- How investing in a blueprint for saleability produces results

---

[42] Murray, WH *The Scottish Himalaya Expedition*, JM Dent & Sons 1951

And what of PSWA? If they follow the blueprint, will they achieve their valuation goal of $15 - $20 million? In fact, Peter did lead his other shareholders through a similar action blueprint. At the beginning of the process, when we met Peter and his company, PSWA had a valuation of $6 - $8 million. This amount left a gap of $9 - $14 million between what the shareholders really wanted and the reality of what their company was really worth.

Peter got help from exit-planning advisors to find out how to reach their goals and resolve their profitability mysteries. He gained buy-in from his shareholders by working with coaches to help him face the hard facts; and, face the reality about how they communicated and ran their business, as well as helping their twenty-three managers learn how to become accountable to strategic goals, new roles and responsibilities. Peter even instituted performance reviews on his shareholders (who also wore functional hats), so that they walked their talk.

When Peter and his shareholders at PSWA stabilized their operation, they increased profitability and they were able to take on larger projects within a dynamic and sought after industry. Soon they were courted as an acquisition target by private and public companies much larger than they were, including past competitors.

While PSWA had a good reputation and talented people working for them, it was their connections and clients in this industry that attracted the interest from acquirers.

PSWA won loyalty from the market place for solving some difficult technical problems that the acquirer couldn't produce in-house. PSWA had become the go-to company in their market niche. After eighteen months of debate, stabilization, optimization, growth, due diligence and nail biting, PSWA shareholders finally got their desired exit. A firm ten times their size acquired them, and that firm had the resources to help them accelerate their specialty work.

Within eighteen months of working their plan, they had an offer on the table for $22 million from a strategic buyer. And, indeed, like Peter's friend, this buyer called unexpectedly (having done their market research); they heard about the company's improving reputation and unique skill set in an industry that this buyer wanted to access. The acquiring company had tried to expand into this industry in the past, but had been unsuccessful. They saw an opportunity to break this losing streak with an acquisition and PSWA fit the bill.

It took a year for PSWA to become stable, and then another year to go from first introduction to final closing. They had to work hard through the distraction of the deal process to keep applying their action blueprint.

Now the next transition starts. Peter, Walter, Andrea and Simon are no longer shareholders. They are employees reporting to a remote boss. However, they are even more accountable than when they owned the company because part of their deal involved an earn-out. They will have to perform to high standards to get the entire $22 million. But, even if they miss the mark, however disappointing that might be, they were still successful in closing the valuation gap in a relatively short two years. Now they must work at re-stabilizing the company to meet the expectations of their new owner.

How would you feel in Peter's shoes? When we first met him, he was frustrated and uncertain in facing the fact that his company was worth $7 million – or $10 million less than the number he'd thrown out to his partners. Not an enviable position. And he had to deal with the news that the company was un-saleable even at that low valuation. Two years later, Peter has gone through a lot of changes and tough issues. But, he has $5 million in the bank and more coming if he does what he has to over the next two years. And his 250 employees have a bright future, too.

Where to you want to be two or three years from now? The journey isn't for the faint of heart. But if that describes you, you wouldn't be reading this book! You are already a successful business owner. Now you want to be just as successful at handing over the reins to the next owner, so they have a polished jewel honed to give them success, too.

That will be the strongest legacy you can leave for all.

About the Authors

Lorraine McGregor has written many articles on how to prepare a business for sale, as well as advising owners in manufacturing, distribution, professional services, software, retail, construction, development and real estate, about how to grow, acquire and sell their companies. She founded Spirit West Management, a management consulting firm, in 1990 with partner and husband, Rob McGregor. Wanting to broaden the number of companies they could serve with their unique and innovative program, they launched the first online training site, www.MakeYourBusinessSaleable.com, to provide ideas, training, and advice for the business owner contemplating a future exit. Lorraine holds a Masters Degree in Business Administration and is the former President of Unitrol America Computer Corporation.

In addition, Lorraine served as President (two years) and Director of the Association for Corporate Growth (ACG Vancouver Chapter) for eight years, the leading association for mergers and acquisitions professionals, as well as deal makers in North America.

Having co-founded a software development company and raised more than $1 million, Lorraine understands what it takes to grow a business and to face and make the critical decisions that shape the future. From advising and working alongside more than 100 companies, she recognizes the organizational patterns that aid and stifle growth, performance and the customer experience. She uses this knowledge, together with partner Rob McGregor, to develop methodologies and tool sets to uncover and remedy these roadblocks.

Clients of all sizes benefit from Lorraine's ability to lead and facilitate management teams through the rocky journey of making the changes that she and Rob recommend in this book. She encourages them to focus on the drivers that will get them what they really want, from growth through preparation for sale or integration after acquisition. Successful exit strategy projects include Illinois Tool Works, The WestBend Company, Wild Oats and Capers Community Markets, and many private companies that must remain confidential.

Rob McGregor is the author of *Followership Intelligence: How to Lead so Others Can Follow*, and he is a co-author of The Leadership Quarterly's *Exploring Social Constructions of Followership: A Qualitative Study*, published by Elseveier, Inc. He holds a BA in Psychology, a Masters in Divinity, a Masters in Business Administration and a Certificate in Conflict Resolution. At the age of twenty-four, he talked his way into a position as a budget officer for a large government department and proceeded to show his superiors how to do the job in a way they never thought possible – to provide service where it was really needed while trimming costs. His methods were completely unorthodox and the department hadn't considered them previously. His superiors were in shock when he delivered a balanced government budget and increased service throughout all departments. His secret? Collaborative discussion and decisions coupled with coaching and education.

For the last twenty years, Rob has coached leaders, CEOs from private companies, to military commanders and their leadership teams. He shows them how to have the types of conversations that free organizations from years of stymied decision-making and productivity-draining paralysis. His innovative style and empathetic (yet tough) approach with even the most hard-nosed business owners has won him many fans over the years.

He believes the key to business success is having the types of conversations that most people never dreamed may be possible. Rob is a master at helping owners, partners, managers and employees find the courage to say what needs to be said. It is the entry point to change and the precursor to profitability.

Lorraine and Rob work with clients across North America from their office in Vancouver, Canada. When not working, they spend their time enjoying the west coast lifestyle.

Spirit West Management, Ltd. is in the business of helping companies grow to the next level so they can stabilize, acquire other firms or sell. Our mission in life is to help companies be powerful sources of economic rejuvenation in their communities.

We are all powerful contributors to economic renewal, so please join the fight.

Begin by scheduling your next steps.

Best of luck on your journey!

Appendix
Gross Margin by Industry and Profit Margin by Industry

What are the typical gross margins and profit margins in your industry? What should you aim for in order to be attractive to investors and financially sound?

Financial Projections.com offers free income statement industry data: http://research.financialprojections.com/IndustryStats-Name

The data provides a breakdown of the income statement and the percent of sales that each line item represents. The data is based on averages and only accounts for one year. The breakdown includes totals for Gross Margin, Total Personnel, Total Expenses, and Net Profit. The industry data may not be perfectly accurate for your business, but it does provide a great foundation for building.

http://biz.yahoo.com/p/sum_qpmd.html

Compare your company to the industry average for each income statement line item.

Income statement statistics by industry:
http://research.financial-projections.com/IndustryStats-GrossMargin

If you want a more detailed report on your industry, try BizMiner. You can buy single industry profiles for a one-time report. Subscriptions are not necessary.

http://www.bvmarketdata.com/defaulttextonly.asp?f=Bizminer

Who is Buying Businesses Such as Mine?

When you are ready to select the type of acquirer you want to hunt, use the Axial Market Tool to search who is buying companies like yours. Recommend it to your advisors, too, and then work together on making contact with appropriate buyers.

https://www.axialmarket.com/selling-a-company/what-is-axialmarket/

What Multiples are Paid in My Industry?

There are many resources for private company comparable sales. For your purposes, BizBuySell at:

http://www.bizbuysell.com/business-valuation-report/ will give you a report in your geographic area and industry for a fee of between $19.95 and $59.95. The database will ask for your gross income, not your EBITDA. Gross Income is your Revenue less your cost of goods sold, but before any other expenses. EBITDA includes the subtraction of other expenses. Their database will calculate a suggested asking price based on the median of the Multiples paid in your area for similar businesses over the last year. Remember, only use this information as a rule of thumb, so you can Handle Reality. When it's time for an actual valuation, let your M&A advisor guide this process.

Where to Get Support for Making Changes?

The Exit Planning Institute to find an advisor to guide you through the entire process https://www.exit-planning-institute.org/.

Financial analysis is what is needed to make smart financial decisions. Look for a Certified Management Consultant CMA, CPA or CA.

Teach your managers how to be financially responsive by taking them through the Profit Adventure game at http://www.profitadventure.com.

Learn how to make better pricing decisions at http://www.EndeavorIQ.com.

To find advisors expert in the mergers and acquisition process to help with legal, accounting, tax and wealth management strategies go to http://www.acg.org and talk to your banker who has many resources in their network.

What to Do Post Exit?

Reading list:

Leap!: What Will We Do with the Rest of our Lives
by Sara Davidson

You Could Live a Long Time. Are you Ready?
by Lyndsay Green

Gonna Jump? – Take a Parachute!: Harnessing Your Power of Choice by David F. McSpadden which shows you how to make the rest of your life, the best of your life.

Want more active learning? Learn how to repurpose who you are:

www.transitioningyourself.com

Thinking you're too old for a next act? Think again!

http://www.RethinkAge.com

Do you want to test out some new career ideas or just try a completely different life experience where you can give people the gift of your wisdom and experience?

www.backdoorjobs.com, www.vocationvacations.com
www.ceso-saco.com

Table of Figures

Here is an overview of the big picture and some of the activities involved . . . (Fig. 7), *5 Phases of an Exit*, Pg. 142.

But first, in order to understand how improving operational effectiveness can increase what a buyer is willing to offer in an acquisition, look at the Multiple Effect table below . . . (Fig. 8), *The Multiple Effect*, Pg. 164.

If Vince and Paul expand their service sales efforts with a growth plan, they can negotiate that additional point on the Multiple. (Fig. 9), *From Un-Saleable to Saleable*, Pg. 170.

Table of Exercises

Bibliography

Advanced Performance Institute. (2011, January 1). *Key Performance Indicators*. Retrieved May 15, 2011 from API: http://www.ap-institute.com/key%20Performance%20Indicators.html

Avery, R. (2006). *The Ten Trillion Dollar Question: A Philanthropic Game Plan.* Cornell, NY, USA: Cornell University.

Axial Market. (2011, May 3). *Private Equity and Strategic Buyers - A Distinction Without a Difference?* Retrieved May 15, 2011 from Business Insider Clusterstock Contrributors: http://businessinsider.com/private-equity-and-strategic-buyers-a-distinction-without-a-difference-2011-5

Belasco, J. A. (1994). *Flight of the Buffalo: Soaring to Excellence, Learning to Let Employees Lead.* New York, NY, USA: Granc Central Publishing.

BMO Financial Group. (2010). *BMO NOrth Amercia Business Sudy: Canadian Business Owners More Upbeat on Economy thatn US Counterparts.* BMO Bank. Toronto: BMO Financial Group.

Bruce, D. D. (2005). *Succession Can Breed Success.* Canadian Federation of Independent Business. Toronto: Canadian Federation of Independent Business.

Capital IQ. (2011). *January 2011 Market Observations: High-level Perspectives of Public Equite, Credit Markets, Private Capital M&A and More"*. McGraw-Hill Companies, Inc, Capital IQ. New York: McGraw-Hill Companies.

Carsten, M. K.-B. (2010, 21). Exploring Social Constuctions of Followership: A Qualitative Study. *The Leadership Quarterly* , 543-562 Elsevier, Inc. Waltham, MA.

Cialdini, R. (1984). *Influence.* New York, NY, USA: HarperCollins Publishers, Inc.

Deans, T. W. (2008). *Every Family's Business.* Orangeville, ON, Canada: Detente Financial Press.

DiFranco, J. (2011, January 1). The Fine Line Between Love and Fear: Exploring the Relationship Between Enetrepreneurs and Private Equity. *Timely Topics for Private Equity.*

Follett, M. P. (1940). *Dynamic Administration: The Collected Papers of Mary Parker Follett.* New York, NY, USA: Harper & Brothers Publishers.

Hsieh, T. (2010). *Delivering Happiness: A Path to Profits, Passion and Purpose.* New York, NY, USA: Business Plus Hachette Book Group.

Kami, M. J. (1994). Don't Reform - Transform. *Management Master* Vol *1* Productivity Press, New York, NY

Leonetti, J. (2010). *Business Exit Strategy Planning: A Growth Niche*. Retrieved March 15, 2011 from www.pinnacleequitysolutions.com: http://www.pinnacleequitysolutions.com/public/107/print.cfm

Maxwell, J. (2004). *Today Matters:Twelve Daily Practices to Guarantee Tomorrow's Success.* New York, NY, USA: Center Street Publishing.

McAskill, T. (2009, January 15). *Identifying Strategic Buyers: Who Can Fully Exploit the Acquisition.* From Invest to Exit: http://www.investtoexit.com/articles/strategic-buyers.html

Murray, W. H. (1951). *The Scottish Himalaya Expedition.*London, England: JM Dent & Sons.

Naisbitt, J. P. (1990). *Megatrends:2000.* New York, NY, USA: Avon Books.

Packer, T. (2011, March 8). *Some States Try to Harness the Economic Power of Immigrant Entrepreneurs.* Retrieved March 9, 2011 from Immigration Impact: http://immigrationimpact.com/2011/03/08/some-states-try-to-harness-the-economic-power-of-immigrant-entrepreneurs

Patterson, K. J. (1976). *Crucial Conversations: Tools or Talking When Sakes are High.* New York, NY, USA: McGraw-Hill.

Pietz, J. (2011, February 7). *The Graying of Chicago - Crane's Business.* Retrieved March 1, 2011 from www.CranesBusiness.com: http://www.chicagobusiness.com/article/20110205/issueo1/302059982/crains-special-report-the-graying-of-chicago#axzz1DyCh44ZaFebruary 7, 2011

Poza, E. (2003, August 11). Heirs and Graces in Family Busiess. *Business Week .*

Quinn, D. (1992). *Ishmael: An Adventure of the Mind and Spirit.* New York, NY, USA: Bantam/Turner.

Rath, T. (2007). *Strengths Finder 2.0.* New York, NY, USA: Gallup Press.

Senge, P. (1990). *The Fifth Discipline: The Art and Practice of the Learning Organization.* New York, NY, USA: Doubleday.

The Gallup Organization. (2011, January 1). *Employee Engagement: A Leading Indicator of Financial Performance.* Retrieved May 15, 2011 from Gallup Consulting: http://www.gallup.com/consulting/52/employee-engagement.aspx

Turock, A. (2002). *Invent Business Opportunities No One Else Can Imagine.* Darby, PA USA: Diane Publishing Co.

US Census Bureau. (2002, September 15). *Survey of Business Owners 2002 - Characteristics of Business Owners.* Retrieved December 12, 2010 from www.Censsus.Gov: http://www.Census.gov/econ/sbo/02/cbosof.html

Workforce. (2011, January 1). *Questions to Measure Employee Engagement.* Retrieved May 15, 2011 from Workforce Topics and Tools: http//home.workforce.com